The Adrenalin Junkies

*A Memoir of the South African Reserve Police
Force in Durban 1979 to 1997*

Douglas Wade

Copyright © 2020 by D N Wade

All rights reserved. This book or any portion thereof may not be reproduced or used in any manner whatsoever without the prior express written permission of the publisher except for the use of brief quotations in a book review, or an academic thesis submitted for a degree at a recognised university

First printing 2019

ISBN 978-1-913340-66-7 (ebook) 978-1-913340-67-4

Published by D N Wade at theadrenalinjunkies@gmail.com

Photo Credits (where known)

Google illustration numbers 1, 2 & 5
D N Wade illustration numbers 12 - 15
G Hamshire illustration numbers 16 -20

Typeset by Geoff Fisher in 12/14.5pt Palatino Linotype

Contents

1. A Policeman's Lot 1
2. Background 5
3. Some of the People 24
4. Streetsweeping 34
5. Working with Other Bodies 94
6. The City Police 109
7. Happiness is Point Charge Office 114
8. Whores 124
9. Training 134
10. Traffic 159
11. The Sporting Life 174
12. Police College 186
13. Childrearing 194
14. The 94 Election 199
15. Appendix: Notes on Pronounciation and Language 207

List of Illustrations

1 The old Central Police Station
2 The new Magistrates' Courts and C R Swart Square
3 View of Central Durban and Esplanade
4 City Centre in about 1910
5 Point Police Station
6 View of Point and the Bluff
7 Dock Gates in the 1920s/1930s
8 Addington hospital when new
9 1970s beach Scene
10 1990s beach Scene
11 Greyville Racecourse
12 My medals
13 Award for 10-Year Medal
14 Award of Honorary Commission
15 Reserve Candidate Officers' Course 7-18 August 1989
16 1994 election: Day 1
17 1994 election: Van Crew
18 1994 Election: Parading On: Day 2
19 1994 election: Guard Unit, Isithebe School
20 1994 election: Guard Unit, near Isithebe

FOREWORD

I JOINED THE SOUTH African Reserve Police Force in 1979 in Durban. I was then a practising attorney and aged 32. Both of these were unusual: as far as I know there were no more than half a dozen attorneys among the ten thousand or more members countrywide, and most members joined before they turned 25.

This memoir tries to give an accurate impression of what it was like for me to be a member of the force in the 18 years until 1997. In part I have been motivated to tell this tale for my grandchildren and their friends for whom this time and place will seem wholly foreign.

I make no particular pretension to academic rigour, political correctness, or lack of personal bias. In writing it I have tried to give a series of accurate snapshots of incidents and people that I recall and to give some context to these as I saw it at that time. As these have evolved from the stories funny or unfunny that I have so generously regaled anyone with a sympathetic or captive ear over the years, they are largely brief. I have also tried to avoid, but not with complete success, the grandfather's old ram approach. It is about the reasonably ordinary but public spirited people who made up the reserve. If some of the events do not conform with popular preconceptions and thus seem strange even surreal, believe me this is what really happened. While I have used English throughout bear in mind that Afrikaans and Zulu were in constant use by nearly all members, and all three were distorted by a range of accents dialects and slang. For that reason some speech will have non-English idioms and rhythms.

I must also thank my daughter Fiona for urging the importance of the context, for proofreading the script and for her zealous advocacy of the humble comma.

I dedicate this account to my fellow adrenalin junkies.

Douglas Wade
(sometime captain S A Reserve Police)
Sevenoaks 2019

Chapter 1

A POLICEMAN'S LOT

"Is there an exit wound?"

"No."

"Good."

He had been a small slight man. He now lay on his right side, his face on the tarmac of the loading bay, a small pile of old clothes filled by a grey body. The bullet hole was on the left of his head near the back. There was very little blood, just a trickle behind his ear. He was still bruising around the eyes.

"That saves us a real schlep looking for the bullet." I looked around. This was not a good site to search. Under the shopping centre two sides and the roof were concrete, two open, with a tarmac floor and room for six to ten trucks.

"Any witnesses?"

"Ja, a couple of outs from that place." Godfrey gestured at Camden Place, a three-storey block opposite. This was well known to us. The building was let as rooms. We reckoned that at any given time there would be at least three rooms selling dagga and mandrax. If we were bored we could always raid it following our noses, sniffing at the keyholes. The occupants were unlikely to get overdrafts, or even credit at the corner cafe.

"Murder and Robbery?"

"They're sending someone – he should be here soon. I've also called the mortuary van. They reckon to be here in under an hour. They're picking up a stiff in Umlazi."

It was a sunny Saturday afternoon. I'd dropped in at the Point Charge Office to see who was working and to make sure they had everything under control. Godfrey Hamshire was the sergeant in charge with a couple of constables doing crime prevention in plain-clothes. They'd been first on scene and taken control. Once the man from Murder and Robbery arrived they handed control of the scene to him. He was a D/Sgt Buthelezi who had worked with some of us before and had confidence in our abilities. He arrived a bit after me, so Hamshire briefed him before the mortuary guys arrived in their gumboots, long gloves and rubber aprons pulling their steel stretcher. Once they'd done their takeaway, we decided to investigate and try to arrest the killer.

Godfrey – whose nickname was Little Godfrey as he was 6' 4" and fairly large – had managed to get a street name of the gunman plus a reasonable description. He got a direction to a flat he possibly might be at. We came up the stairs to the fourth floor avoiding the lift. The flat was opposite the lift and stairs. There were now five of us with Ben Lenz and Roland Dunstan, all armed of course but only with pistols. Before going into the flat we squatted with our backs to the outer wall spread each side of the door but avoiding windows. Buthelezi was around the corner. We drew and cocked. Godfrey was about to knock, but then voices came up the stairs. We waited. Three young Black men wandered casually up, saw us, but did not break stride or hesitate in their chat, totally ignored five armed men, and carried on up the stairs. We grinned at each other. Then Godfrey knocked.

An Indian woman opened the door. Godfrey told her we were looking for a criminal, ID'ed himself, and asked to search the flat. She agreed, so we moved in rapidly pistols in hand. We looked through the rooms greeting the other occupants. In the bedroom we asked her to open the wardrobes while Roly and I covered them one from each side. Someone was apparently asleep on a bed with the sheet over his head. Roly and I were each side of the foot of the bed covering the figure. I asked her to pull down the sheet, which she did. A tousled Indian man's head appeared. He woke, opened his eyes, looked at the two muzzles pointing straight at him, muttered "Oh, bloody police," rolled over, and pulled the sheet back over his head. We had to laugh, as did the others once we were back on the stairs.

Our next visit was to a party in the next block. Godfrey and Buthelezi chatted to some of the largely Black crowd. They knew our quarry. He'd been there earlier. He was sleeping in a room in a nearby parking garage. It was now dark.

Belmont Arcade had two floors of shops then three parking levels and above that a tower block of 14 storeys of flats. The bottom parking level had no rooms. The second did. We walked very quietly through checking some storerooms and a couple of second hand toilets. It was now past ten pm. The lighting was minimalist and slowed by the humidity. The sleeping room was reached up a short flight of broken irregular concrete steps. At the top a passage led off to the right. It was about a metre wide and six metres long leading to a wooden door which filled the end. It seemed to be jammed against the opening from the inside. We drifted away and considered. The killer was presumably in there armed and happy to shoot. The door would not stop a bullet. The passage could be a deathtrap with ricochets off floor, walls and ceiling, all concrete. How many men were in there and how armed we did not know.

We cocked our pistols, turned off the safety catches. Godfrey went up to the door on the right hand side and flattened himself against the wall. Ben who was the smallest made himself very small at the foot of the door on the left aiming to fire up through the door. Roly and I stood round the corners at the other end of the passage aiming right and left handed at the door. Buthelezi was behind me, watching us with interest. Godfrey reached across and started to knock on the top left corner of the door Zulu-style softly and repeatedly. He then started in a rambling, slurred high-pitched Zulu. "Is Sipho there? I am Siyabonga and we, we were drinking together only on Monday, or was it Tuesday, but he, he had money and he bought. A good man. Sipho?"

From inside came: "There is no Sipho here, you drunken idiot. We're sleeping."

"No no, Sipho said that he was here in this place and I promised him we would drink together again, but …"

"Go away. Fuck off," again from inside.

" … I would pay and now I have been paid, and, I have now the money so Sipho …"

At this the door was plucked back by a large Black and angry man. Godfrey shoulder-charged the door and the man back across into the far wall. Ben jumped in covering that man and another in a bed to the left. Roly and I charged down the passage and in, covering to right and left and followed by Buthelezi. Two more men were in beds to the right. All four were spread-eagled facing the wall. We searched the beds. Godfrey found a pistol under one pillow and handed it to Buthelezi. IDs were checked and Nqutu was the man sleeping on the pistol. He was immediately handcuffed and taken out. Buthelezi reckoned the others were harmless; certainly he and his colleagues weren't looking for them.

Soon, there were two developments. The seized pistol proved to be the murder weapon. Nqutu got bail of R500 or five clips, about four days' wages for a middling secretary. He went back to work, running a security company's armoury.

When Godfrey told me this he bet me all the witnesses would duck and Nqutu would walk.

He was right.

Chapter 2

BACKGROUND

I joined the SA Reserve Police in 1979 at the old Durban Central police station. This was in reaction to the 1976 riots which served to redefine and polarise the political scenery. A lot of people joined the commandos for local service. One friend of mine, a lecturer in classics, found himself guarding electrical substations near Lamontville in the middle of the night. This really didn't appeal to me.

Most Natal and Cape regiments had started as volunteer corps in Victorian times, while the old republics had a call on anyone from 16 to 65 to join local commandos. In 1910 the new Union Defence Force was modelled on the Swiss system of a citizens' army, but dropped the old republican idea of voting for their officers. By the time I left school in 1965 nearly all white men were called up for military service for a nine-month spell plus refresher camps. I was exempted but for the next twenty-five years nearly everyone barring cripples served for up to two years. There were volunteer Coloured, Black and Indian units.

There was a long tradition of volunteering for the services. In the country as a whole, only volunteers served in the world wars. My grandfather was a member of the Town Guard in Dundee in the 1914 war, which started with a minor civil war against the rebels under some of the old Boer generals. On the government side this was the first campaign fought using primarily motor vehicles. In the 1939 war, while a bank manager, he was a special constable in Pinetown. In the siege of Ladysmith, in the Anglo-Boer war, four great-great-uncles of my children were involved: George Newlands in the Natal Carbineers inside, George Neal in the British forces under Buller, and two Fourie brothers in the Ermelo commando doing the besieging. Even Gandhi, then a Durban advocate, raised and commanded as a sergeant-major a company of Indian stretcher-bearers that served under Buller. All the younger attorneys and articled clerks in my firm were officers in the services, bar Allan who was only a corporal, but he had not deferred his service till after university. The bloke with whom I split the transport of our sons to school, was a consulting anaesthetist and a Lt Col, OiC of a SAAF reserve fighter squadron. His great-uncle, a Cdr Dunning, had been the first pilot to land successfully on a Royal Naval ship, a cruiser with a deck on top of a gun turret.

*

Initially I tried to join the local civil defence run by the city council, but that proved to be a total shambles run by a confused man who committed suicide. I then turned to the police. Even there I ended up signing three or four sets of applications as they were faulty or lost. Then it turned out that I had to put up six referees as I was not born in South Africa. I did but picked people of good standing and of influential families that had been at varsity with me, scattered all over the country. After a few months, I got a number of puzzled queries along the line of "What have you been up to? The Security Police have just called …"

Mind you, I may have been given special treatment as other foreign-born members had no idea of this requirement. At Stellenbosch University I quite possibly had a Special Branch file. Certainly one friend of mine, whose father had been the

Aktuaris of the NGK's general synod – in other words one of the top four churchmen holding office in the overall synod of that church – walked into the local security police office and asked to see his file. He saw it was rather thick, though they did not let him read it.

*

I should perhaps remark that the force was multiracial, as was the regular force, of which about half were blacks. All ranks were open to all races, male and female, though this was evolving during my time. The first female reservists were recruited in 1981, and the first female lieutenants were promoted some ten years later. They held active command, not staff posts. To avoid confusion, at that time the police consisted of the SAP, the regular force; the SAP Reserve, which consisted of former members of the SAP who could be recalled for so-called camps of a month or so's duration; and the SA Reserve Police, which were the volunteers. We normally joined at a station in the area we lived or worked or at least one nearby. As a result, we commonly stayed far longer at a specific station than did the regulars, who were often moved to avoid over-comfortable relations with the locals. Later, in the 1990s, the SAP became the SA Police Service.

*

Politics was not a subject discussed among us. That is not to say that we did not have political opinions. One would have had to be brain-dead not to have an opinion in a country where politics started with the questions, where is the country and who are its citizens? It would be fair to say that we were conservatives, in the English small c sense, but also that we were sceptical of politicians and their Procrustean ideologies. On a personal level, I had a slightly different perspective as I had been six years in a small rural primary school in Scotland, where nearly all my fellow pupils were the children of working men, farmhands and the like – jobs done almost exclusively in South Africa by blacks, or in the Western Cape largely by Coloureds.

*

In the first two years I did very little except turn up at the monthly meetings. As I was an attorney they thought I was one of the enemy, so I was never asked out on operations – which left me wondering what exactly they were trying to hide. The first crowd control job I did was for the military parade through the city centre in 1981 for the twentieth anniversary of the Republic. I was given a set of handcuffs, a whistle and a baton, and told to wear a jacket and tie. This was the last such parade: they died of apathy.

*

I served all my time in the centre of Durban, a city of about three million people. Of these about 350 000 were white, probably at least 80% English speaking, though there were many Afrikaans speakers; some 800 000 or so were Indian, also English speakers, though the grandparents often spoke Hindi or Tamil at home; another 50 000 or so were coloured, while the balance of 1 800 000 or more were black, overwhelmingly Zulu. There were also quite sizable groups of Portuguese, Mauritians, Germans, and Greeks, but the common language was English. Religion was mixed too. The largest groups were Christian, Hindu and Moslem. Christians ranged from Catholics and all the usual European churches, shading into animist groups. About 570 churches were recognised in the country. Among the more visible of these African churches were the Ebenezers, who danced and sang in green robes in the parks and streets on Sundays and feast days. Most Buddhists were of course Chinese.

*

Society was filled with various forms of prejudice. The city was very much an English creation, with few Afrikaners there save those working for the civil service or the railways, until say the 1960s, so there was an imperial and colonial mindset described by the wife of the governor-general in about 1930 as "delightfully middle class".

*

Before the Union in 1910, there had been one rather forgotten category of people in Natal, the emancipated native. Broadly, as I understand it, they had to be literate in English and living in a European and Christian style. They then qualified for the vote and could own land as an individual, as opposed to the tribesmen who occupied communal land allocated by their chief or induna in terms of customary law. I came across them in title deeds when registering servitudes over smallholdings in Groutville, an old mission station near Stanger. The Christian natives centred on Groutville elected their own chief, who was for several years Chief Luthuli. This assimilation system was eliminated by the Treaty of Union, so there were in all less than two hundred of them.

In the interwar years the racial question had nothing to do with the Blacks; it was about British and Boers. Some of the biggest political battles of the 1920s were fought over the flag. Blacks in those days did not live on a permanent basis in the cities and towns in great numbers. That started around 1945 with the increase in manufacturing stimulated by war production. In the early 1960s the English, who then still applauded the royal family when they appeared on the movie newscasts, thought condescendingly of Afrikaners as largely lower class, of Indians as clever but pushy, and of Blacks as simple but happy country types. This, broadly, was an adaptation of English class snobberies, with the Afrikaners and Blacks to some extent playing the role of the working class, and the Indians that of the cunning Levantines. This was helped by the fact that since about 1870 labouring or working-class British had been actively discouraged from emigrating to the Cape and Natal. The Afrikaners did not enjoy being condescended to, especially as they were in the process of throwing off the "poor white" image and reality: partly through political action with the National Party, which was essentially a socialist party; partly by creating their own financial, manufacturing and mining companies; and partly by education. Political loyalties ran on tribal lines, not class divisions, and the shadow of the Boer War, or the *Tweede Vryheidsoorlog*, had a real impact until the 1960s, when the declaration of the Republic and departure from the Commonwealth satisfied a longheld political aim. To get an idea of the longterm bitterness behind this, you had only to look at the war memorials in the old Republics, which, at Ermelo for instance, had one column for battle casualties, and one with far more names on it for the women and children dead in the concentration camps. When I was about to leave school in 1965 my housemaster's jaw literally dropped when I told him I was going to Stellenbosch University. My generation was the first that mixed to any great extent.

This left the English-speakers in an uneasy limbo where they relied on the Nationalists to control things, while they could pretend they had nothing to do with it. They had economic power but no real political influence, though their main party, the United Party, was in many ways just as right-wing as the Nationalists. This divide had been exacerbated during the Second World War when the United Party under Smuts, which supported the British side, locked up most of the leading Nationalists as security risks as being sympathetic to the Germans. As a result, during the 1947 royal tour Verwoerd, then editor of the *Transvaaler* newspaper, only warned of the road closures when the royals came to Pretoria. At school I remember having to write a paper comparing the National Party with the Nazis.

On the other hand, a couple of masters were quite shocked by a liberal old boy who sat, not in the back, but in the front seat of his car next to his black driver. Ironically they would have expected a black passenger to be in the back, though I would have thought that showed the black to be the superior and the white the chauffeur. Mind you, until the 1960s non-whites could use the back two or three seats upstairs in the trolley buses in Durban. The railway buses had a small first-class compartment of six or eight seats next the driver. When I was going in one from Paulpietersburg to Mbabane, I rode in solitary splendour with four new tyres up to the border. There I was joined from the back by a Durban Indian student and a Swazi sub-inspector of police, who promptly interrogated the Indian about what he was doing. Indians then were only allowed to stay in Swaziland for 72 hours without a permit.

The biggest and potentially most violent racial divide in Durban was not that between Afrikaners and Blacks, but between Blacks and Indians. The Zulus despised the Indians and thought of them, probably as they had never fought a real war against them, as soft targets. In 1949 there had been major riots in Durban with many Indians killed by Zulus and this remained a strong folk memory. "They ran like rabbits," was a common tale. Even in the 1980s, much of the Cato Manor area a few miles to the south-west of the city centre was a wasteland, with a string of Indian houses and shops along the road, after the Black shacks were removed after the 1960 riots. In January 1960 in Cato Manor a police patrol against illegal brewers was attacked by a mob and nine members stoned and hacked to death and others injured. That is partly why the police at Sharpeville were trigger happy. In the 1976 disturbances the Indians spontaneously set up armed groups to defend the boundaries of their suburbs against any invasions from nearby Black areas, while at the same time their left-wing activists were cheering on the ANC. Inside the police, the black members were often not happy to be commanded by Indians, though they would accept Whites. One illuminating incident happened when an Indian major was sent to be the station commander at Inanda, a former KZP station. On the first day, they refused even to let him through the perimeter fence; on the second, after a direct order from District, they let him in but totally ignored him, not even giving him a cup of tea.

The central area was traditionally and legally white-owned, save for the Grey Street area in the CBD which was Indian. This survived thirty years of Group Areas legislation which would have made it white, by various legal ruses such as unending delays in winding up estates, or the use of white nominees, who ironically were often Afrikaners. As time passed, this system atrophied and died even before the laws had been repealed, so that by 1994 all the old Group Areas had effectively vanished. At least one of our Indian members was living on the Esplanade before that became strictly speaking legal, but we just shrugged.

The old Central police station was an ageing and sweaty building with sagging wooden floors; it was once used as a hospital, and, after the police left, as an army command post. It lay towards the inland end of West Street, a block or two from the big banks and shops. It was very much not a custom-built station. The Charge Office was shoehorned into a large ordinary room next the entrance, which was a single door. A counter had been built across the room, divided on the public side, as was then the custom, by a partition into white and non-white sides, each with a single entry door. In the side wall to the rear was a door that led into the grill, simply a large steel cage, the size of a small room, bolted to the wall of the building and the ground. That door was steel-reinforced and secured by a stout hasp, with a serving spoon dropped in to hold it. Unfortunately there was only one counter-flap, on the white side. That meant that any violent black arrestee had to be dragged in through the front door, then through the black door to be processed, then out the black door into the white door, through the counter across a space crammed with desks and chairs, and finally into the grill. Luckily there was an outside door to the grill for the takeaways; unluckily the wall was not soundproof.

Once I became fed up with doing nothing, I learned the basics of Charge Office work in that hectic little room from our then branch commander a Lt Len Barker. He was a plain genuine guy who'd grown up in Molteno. He took me in personally, coached me and made for me the useful social links with the regular Warrant Officers who ran the shifts.

The area of the old Central station basically covered the town as it existed in, say, 1860, plus a bit of the beach. It bordered on Somtseu Road station to the north, Berea which included Greyville racecourse to the west, Durban Bay to the south up to Congella (which fell under Umbilo) and Maydon Wharf (then an SA Railways Police station covering the port area), and Point to the south-east. Over the years the Railways Police were absorbed into the SAP, and the Central and Somtseu Road areas were amalgamated to form C R Swart Square's area, which stretched north to the Umgeni River. The Railways Police was reckoned by many as an inferior force held together by its Black NCO's. The nickname for their constables was "blompotte", that is, flowerpots, as they sat in the sun on railway platforms, but to the serious irritation of the SAP earned distinctly more than them.

The district and divisional offices and other facilities of the SAP were then scattered all over town. I frankly never knew where half of them were, not that I needed to. In about 1980/1 C R Swart Square was built, a tower block with the Station itself on the ground and first floors, the Security Police in the top three floors, Radio Control on the eleventh floor, and District and Divisional Headquarters in the eight or so floors below that. The garages, stores, cells and Dog Unit were out back with lots of parking. On one side was another tower block of police married-quarters flats, on the other the magistrates' courts.

This was fourteen floors high and something of an architectural curiosity, marking the high point of apartheid design. The plan was to have not just a secure prisoner route to all criminal courts from the basement holding cells, which could be reached by an underground tunnel from the cells at the Square, but a complete double access for the public. Whites would go in one entrance on the southern side, Non-Whites in the other on the northern side and they would end up on one or other side of the divided courts in the tower block without meeting. When the locals realised what was intended, they decided to boycott the whole thing, especially the lawyers, and the scheme was abandoned so that everyone could go where they wanted. We did have an awful lot of corridors, stairs and lifts, which was as well as the lift maintenance was not good. I remember once riding in a lift with an inner door missing. Durbanites were rather sensitive about lifts. The Natal Building Society, which had a banana theme for its advertising, once came up with the slogan: "Come into the NBS and get your slice". A week later, in their headquarter building, a lift malfunctioned and a customer was sliced in half. A self-imposed disaster was the slogan "At the NBS we say yes". Before two days had passed, the female staff refused to wear the buttons again.

Until the 1980s, notices of executions relevant to the magisterial district were posted at the magistrates' courts. These showed a photograph of the person hanged and gave details of the victim or victims and the crime, which in practice was nearly always murder. Across the country there were about a hundred each year. Anyone who faced a potential death sentence was given a *pro deo* advocate, generally a junior advocate. I remember about five months into my last year at varsity meeting a guy from the previous year going glumly to the cinema. When asked why so down, he replied that they were hanging the third of his clients the next morning.

I spent ten years at Central and C R Swart Square which was

named after the last governor-general and first state president, but generally called simply the Square. Blackie Swart's farm in the Orange Free State was called *"Die Aap"*, that is, the ape, which led to lengthy debate as to whether the farm sign should read *"Die Aap"* / C R Swart" or "C R Swart / *Die Aap*", but he never renamed the farm. This was, in passing, the only station that had a photograph of a state president on display in it. Every station, though, had a pressed plastic panel showing illustrations of limpet and land mines and other Russian weaponry.

I was made up to Sergeant after three and a half years, to Warrant Officer after six, and finally was invited to the commissioned officers' course in the second half of my tenth year. When I returned, I was asked to take over Point, which was then at rather a low ebb, with only nine members as opposed to the forty or so at the Square. On arrival I promptly fired three inactive, leaving six active members. From there we built up to fifty-plus. I reckoned fifty was as much as we could really cope with, so we winnowed down to under forty three times in the next five years.

Uniforms reflected the history of the force. When I was at school in the 1960s, the workaday summer uniform was a safari suit in tough polyester twill, often with shorts with the so-called bus driver's cap. The white members wore blue, the non-whites khaki. Before I joined, shorts had been dropped and everyone wore blue. Ranks too had become the same for all races, and a steady stream of non-white officers were being promoted primarily in their own areas, especially in the homelands which had separate forces such as the KwaZulu Police. Even so roughly half the SAP was non-white. The ranks were Constable; Lance Sergeant which was an acting rank used mostly to make sure there was someone able to give bail at a Charge Office; Sergeant; Warrant Officer, known previously as Head Constable; Lieutenant; Captain; and then military ranks up to the

Commissioner who was a full General. The homeland forces after 1994 were reincorporated into the SAPS.

When I joined we wore a brown leather Sam Browne belt and holster, with black shoes. The tunic had brass buttons secured for choice by key rings. The seams scratched a bit, and in Durban I often was running with sweat. The winter uniform, which in Durban we only ever wore at formal occasions – I think I wore mine once for a funeral - had a heavy blue cloth jacket and grey trousers. Female members were dressed as secretaries, with jacket, skirt and court shoes, topped with a decorative felt hat, and initially had to carry handbags and wear blue leather gloves. Mind you, the daftest uniform I heard of was from a former member of the Mounted Unit: they found themselves in full riding kit of black serge with solar topee and spurs, walking foot patrols in central Durban in the summer of 1960, then being rushed to the Transkei in trucks wearing white dust coats to keep the dust from the roads off their uniforms.

In the 1980s uniforms became more practical with the introduction of the new summer and field dress types. Summer now had a light blue cotton shirt, the same twill trousers, cap and shoes, but the pistol was now carried on the hip in a webbing belt and holster. We still wore the bus driver's cap which made us easily visible in a crowd, something which can be a real advantage, though at times we would take it off, especially at night to disguise our silhouette. The light blue shirts looked smarter than the later dark blue version which makes one look more like a mechanic. Field dress had canvas boots, light canvas pants and jacket with a cloth cap, and was designed for rough or country use. This, in Durban, was warm enough for a midwinter night shift in the rain. Upcountry, they wore fur liners in the jacket. To keep the front of the cap looking sharp, we generally lined it, ideally with pieces of X-ray plates or stiff plastic sheeting. Unofficially, female members (who previously had slit and tacked a seam in their skirts so they could rip it to move faster) took to the field dress like a flash especially if, say, they were a dog handler. Though the shirts took a lot of damage in fights, they were far more comfortable. Rank badges for sergeants were cloth stripes sewn to the right sleeve of the tunic, plus a metal five-sided castle above them, but later a metal badge was pinned to the shirt. Warrant Officers always had a metal badge on both sleeves. I forgot this when newly promoted and shoulder-charged a door, punching three neat holes in my arm. They also wore a fancy stitched Sam Browne. Officers had cloth shoulder badges for field dress and metal on board for summer.

One irony was that during all the years that South Africa was routinely pilloried overseas as a police state, the police were poorly, if not dreadfully, paid. In about 1972 I was asked to help a black constable in a maintenance case. His gross monthly pay was R49, and after fixed expenses, transport, and deductions including a bed in a police barracks, he was left with R3, which meant that if he wanted to eat he had to be corrupt. R3 then would then have bought you say 30 pies or 10-15 poor quality fish and chips. In the 1980s and 1990s, although members could qualify for civil service housing loans, they of necessity had to live in the cheaper suburbs like Montclair, unless they had a wife with a well-paying job. Many, though, chose to live in police housing as that was far cheaper.

Recruitment of reservists could be instructive. Applicants first applied in writing and could be asked for a medical clearance. Often it was by word of mouth, with existing members bringing in friends or relatives. They were supposed to be literate in English or Afrikaans, and aged between 18 and 70. Anyone over, say, 50 was looked at rather carefully, as it was pointless to have members who had themselves to be guarded. One applicant, apart from age, had a glass eye, which must have been a bit small for the socket, as the lint he packed it with had a habit of creeping out. Physical defects could be accepted but it was a question of whether they could do the job. Perhaps the one exception was one poor woman I refused as she had a squint in her right eye, and the left eye had a continual sideways flutter. If in doubt, we offered an attachment to Radio Control only, which as a rule was refused. Applicants had to be working, to prevent anyone joining for an income. If a member lost his job, his colleagues would often try to find him a new one.

At Point I interviewed the applicants or, if I was too busy, got Nollie van Zyl or Godfrey Hamshire, both Sergeant,s to help out. We called at their homes without notice. That way we met the families, and could assess how enthusiastic they were, and how desirable the applicants were. Curiously, when asked, very few could give any well-articulated reasons for wanting to join.

One Indian member at the Square had gangster relatives. A cousin was caught halfway through a garden fence in Alpine Road with his family holding his body, and his wife and her family holding his head till his mother-in-law used a tomahawk to chop off his head. Our guy happily was reliable, and working outside his home area of Sydenham.

One odd character was a White member at Point. His family and their circumstances all seemed normal at the interview, as did he. However he later proved to be a complete Walter Mitty. He passed himself off as a lieutenant in the Recces, that is, the local Special Forces unit, and as such conned a girl in Pinetown to marry him. Only when he failed to pay the wedding caterers up-front did it collapse. As he was then being investigated for fraud, I went with Godfrey to track him down and detain him, which we did, to save our reputation with the regulars.

The quickest dismissal from the Reserve Police I heard of was of one man who was seen one midday by a couple of passing Reaction Unit members aiming his new revolver up Alice Street, a major street. They promptly shot him twice in the leg. By the time he was released from casualty at tea time Lt Barker and the station commander had fired him, and seized the revolver.

The primary question was always: can I work with this person? An error of judgement could literally kill us; so we took it seriously.

Individual ranks tended to follow work levels. Everyone started as a constable, but most sergeants and Warrant Officers were at least artisans or skilled people, while officers tended to be self-employed businessmen or managerial types. We reckoned constables should be able to put together the paperwork; the sergeants should be able to make sure it was correct; and the Warrant Officers should be able to fake it. In turn the experience and abilities gained in the force, used intelligently, helped members in their careers.

Although members had officially only to work four hours a month, as a rule anyone not doing eight would be dropped. That, after all, needed only one shift and a meeting. I reckoned twenty hours was needed to keep one in practice and develop experience. My average was about forty, but some members regularly beat a hundred. I worked therefore the equivalent of three months' full time in a year. My record was 300 hours, but that was the month I went to the College. Point's highest, for the month of the 1994 election, was over 3 000. Twenty members broke 100.

Promotion to sergeant could take place after three years, to Warrant after another three, to Lieutenant again after three, and to Captain after two. One restriction was that you had to be junior to your station commander. To be a Lieutenant you had to have a unit of at least twenty members. As Point was run by a Major I could not be promoted above Captain without moving to a bigger station or to say District Headquarters. At a small country station, a reservist could seldom rise above Sergeant. In Durban most of the Reserve units were headed by officers, mostly Lieutenants, with a scattering of Captains, a couple of Majors, and a solitary Colonel (then Brigadier), who was our divisional then our provincial officer. The Reserve force was always multi-racial, though the racial composition in any given station tended to follow the demographics of that station's area. Chatsworth was therefore almost wholly Indian, Umlazi just Zulu, but the Square and Point among others were pretty mixed, with Whites and Indians being the two biggest groups, with a number of Coloured and Black members; and after 1981 women again of all races.

At a station level the reservists formed a branch with its commander reporting to the station commander, as would the heads of the uniform and detective branches. At Point at one stage, my station commander was a White Major, the head of detectives an Indian Captain, and the station second in command an Arab Lieutenant. We had the same ranks, uniforms, powers and medals as a regular; but no power of command over regulars. Promotion to Warrant Officer gave the biggest single increase in powers. I could then legally order my troops to open volley fire on a rioting crowd. Promotion to Lieutenant made me a justice of the peace, though that was never used. We did not get any pay, but qualified for medical care and a free funeral. As a result I, even when an officer, could, when working with regular constables, make at best pointed suggestions, and if they did something really stupid or irregular, I'd have a quiet word with the duty officer. He had to attend any police shooting or vehicle collision in the district, plus any other deserving incident. This, though, was rare, partly as our units largely operated independently, but in collaboration with others.

With a few exceptions of reservists attached to the Dog Unit, detectives or Radio, we were all in the uniform branch. There were also some specialised reservists, such as pilots, accountants, or divers who were used for their special skills, but they did not become involved in station activities. Our duties focused around Charge Office, complaints, crowd control or visible policing, all of which were done in uniform; or crime prevention which was done in plain-clothes. Here the general approach was to blend in, watch and hunt criminals. Each month the reservists would take over the station for at least one shift, depending on numbers. This was the theory, but this wasn't always possible at the Square, where security prisoners had to be supervised by a regular sergeant who ran a minor dispensary, so we never ran the cell block which could hold 160. There was also always a shortage of people allowed to carry a shotgun and willing to spend their shift up a concrete guard tower on the perimeter wall, arguably the most boring job in the force, worse even than a hospital guard. I once spent a night in a ward largely full of old bronchial men, listening to near death rattles. Both my prisoner and I found that pretty depressing.

We did run the Square's Charge Office, though only three of us were trusted to be the Charge Office commander. This was because the regular Warrants needed to rely on us for accurate accounting for, and control of, the better part of a hundred firearms, thousands of rounds of ammunition, and hundreds if not thousands, of rand, and much else including the flags, apart from the smooth control of the policing of the whole area. Technically the Charge Office commander was the senior man in the station's area, especially at night, and this was the busiest station in the province. Any cash shortages had to be made good by all the members of the shift out of their own pockets, which happily I never had to do.

I can remember surprising the occasional regular by refusing to accept a charge as the docket was not properly or fully made out. It was a three-ring circus, with perhaps 70 dockets a day being opened by a variety of units, while three phones rang constantly and a steady trickle of people came to the counter.

At least two Charge Office reserves were needed. I can also remember having to hand over to the incoming Warrant at a shift end some 32 prisoners arrested, but not yet in the cells, on charges from urination to murder, matching each one to his docket. Each had to be correctly identified to the incoming Charge Office commander to avoid swapping. It was not unknown for a murderer to make a deal to take the place of a by-law offender, pay an admission of guilt, and leave the other guy to go to court and only then say he was the wrong man.

I ran the unit at Point for five years, which were the best of my time. One frustration was that I had few I could promote for want of time served, so we operated with few NCOs and were thus liable to be invaded by senior members from other stations who could arrive with rank above the old hands. The other was the growing tendency to faction. Some took against others for reasons not always particularly clear. The worst case led to a defamation action being attempted. I had advised that there was no case, but it was only when a leading firm of attorneys came to the same conclusion that the matter was dropped. I also had towards the end a station commander who unusually was not particularly supportive. I was asked to focus on the training role for District 46 so had to leave Point in the hands of an invader Warrant Officer, who soon left. The unit collapsed in a couple of years back to half a dozen amateurs.

When I tried to set up a properly operating training operation that could run a training library on computer discs that could help any unit in Natal, I precipitated a fire fight between two regular outfits about the budget; and not surprisingly got nothing, not even stationery.

I finally felt I had done everything I could. Certainly I had no desire to fight paper wars I could not win. Also the force was being changed radically in tone and effectiveness by a variety of things, largely the installation at senior officer level of ANC cadres often newly returned to the country, and with no real police experience, who now commanded the men they had been trying to kill.

In my resignation letter I quoted T S Eliot: "I grow old, I grow old, / I shall wear the bottoms of my trousers rolled". And so I went.

Chapter 3

SOME OF THE PEOPLE

The Reserve Police had a pretty wide range of people in it, nearly all of whom had well-defined and strong characters. Anyone who did not, simply did not last more than a few hours. You took the job knowing that it could be rough, and at times dangerous, but then any shift could turn into an adventure. The consolation was that you were doing something positive to protect your family and your neighbours. I have therefore tried here to give a thumbnail sketch of some of my colleagues over the years plus a few others to give a flavour of the whole.

Sgt Abel Abraham, an Indian Baptist at the Square, was the most senior Indian electrician with the city council. At his wedding reception, I was chatting to him when a bus arrived from Tongaat and offloaded about forty old aunties, all in their saris. I asked him if they were from his side or his wife's. He had no idea, but then there were already nigh on a thousand guests being served breyani with saucers from tin baths. I was one of a handful of white guests, and was thus the target of quite a few curious looks, until the Rev Timothy, the secretary-general of the Baptist Union, arrived and greeted me as an old acquaintance.

John Baldock was an English member, about 1,93m tall and beefy, who had been in Cape Town where he had served in the Cape Garrison Artillery before moving up. He founded a business brokering the services of Escom trucks on empty return trips after delivering construction materials. He could afford a speed boat and other good stuff until Escom suddenly decided to do the business themselves. He decided that he had no real long term future so he sold up in two months and returned to the UK.

Len Barker was the lieutenant in charge at the old Central and then at the Square. He had grown up in Molteno, in the depths of the Karoo, and in Durban worked as the supervisor of a large block of flats. Two things he said have stuck in my mind. Once in a lecture he asked us, "Which of you is willing to die for your country?" When no-one replied, he responded, "Good, I want you to live for your country." He also liked to say, "There are no stupid questions, only stupid silences."

Athalie Bauer was our first female sergeant at Point. She was a local girl, with her parents working for the SA Railways & Harbours and living near the old dock entrance, and two brothers in the force as regulars at Point. She worked as a secretary in an import / export firm in Congella. She was something of a party girl, but was much tougher and unillusioned than she might have seemed. Her introduction to policing, she once remarked, was on her third day, trying to save a man's life by holding his severed femoral artery shut with her fingertips. That was before the arrival of Aids.

Andrew Bertolotti was the tall, thin son of a Milanese immigrant. As such, he liked to explain the practicalities of the Mafia's system of patronage. He had a liking for the *bella figura*. He had served on the border with the artillery on the G5 batteries. These were locally made 155mm cannon with a range of 40kms, or with booster rounds about 60kms, that we sold to both the Iraqi and Iranian armies during their war. He was not much of a paperwork man, preferring the action on the street.

Busane and Mabaso were the two leading black members in the late 1980s at the Square. Busane was in his thirties, calm, short of speech but diligent. Mabaso was more voluble, and reckless to a degree that I more than once wondered how he had never been killed. He also had a bad habit of failing to reach rendezvous points on time. As Zulu speakers, they rounded out the ability of patrols to talk to anyone, and to get good information. An oddity was a diffident member called Nero who disappeared and was later rumoured to have gone to an ANC training camp in Tanzania.

Jean Carlier was the only reservist I heard of who was awarded a police medal for bravery. This was for clambering some twenty metres down off a road bridge over a broad, fast-flowing river in the Tongaat area, and saving from drowning two Indian canoeists whose craft had capsized. He was Belgian and had done his military service there, in their parachute regiment. When I was asked to present the medal to him he flatly refused to accept it either publicly or privately.

Sgt Chetty, who was at the Square with me, was a high school teacher and later a school principal in East London. His grandfather (who had been major domo to Sir Liege Hulett, probably the richest Victorian sugar farmer in Natal) was buried with his wife in the Hulett family plot. This was, for its time, a remarkable distinction. Chetty certainly did not think himself inferior to anyone, and with good reason. He was about 1.9m tall and had a commanding air.

"Bags" Crookes was the captain in charge at Umzinto where he worked as head of security for Crookes Bros, a major sugar estate owned by millionaire but distant cousins of his. I recall discussing shooting snipe in the Spanish marshes with one of them. The two branches of the family came from two brothers who were youngsters in Umzinto in 1870 when the Kimberley diamond rush started. Both wanted to go but they had just ten shillings between them, only enough for one to go. They drew lots and Bags' great-grandfather won. The loser stayed, married the local blacksmith's daughter, inherited his farm and started the sugar estates.

Capt Chris de Wet was the creator of the shooting range and

training ground up at Tongaat that became known as Dewetskop. He was an estate manager for Tongaat-Hulett there, a major sugar-growing company. He persuaded them to give him the use of a disused quarry and an adjoining river valley, and built shooting ranges, a *lapa* or braai area, showers, and other facilities, with space for parking and lectures. This was a desperately needed facility and was used for practical training of reservists across most of Natal. He was a large, dark-haired, strong and vivid character rather given to throwing hand grenades at trainees. He had a long-term Indian girlfriend whom he married as soon as it became legal. Later he moved to Mozambique to go farming.

Dave Fisher was the officer in charge of the reservists at Berea, ending up a major. The Berea was the old moneyed area, so some of their members had the view that they had a better class of crime. He had the misfortune of his wife running off with another member, which made his life impossible as he had been working for his father-in-law. As he had been a regular, he was both a member of the police reserve as well as the Reserve Police. When he was called up for service in the police reserve, he ranked only as a sergeant, but he arranged to wear his Reserve force rank uniform to avoid anomalies.

Dr Flemming was the most vivid of the many district surgeons I met over the years. She had grown up a German speaker in the Sudetenland area of Czechoslovakia, and studied at the University of Prague. I met her on a number of occasions with drunk drivers. Part of the blood testing procedure was to ask what and when they had eaten and drunk during the previous 24 hours. When one sozzled young Indian admitted to about a bottle of cane spirits plus much else, but only one cheese sandwich in the day, she exclaimed (after nearly breaking his hand on the table when he tried to resist her): "You are a child at drinking! What you need is a haunch of venison roasted with lard and a plate of dumplings. Then you can drink."

Sgt Mari Govender was one of the longest-serving members at the Square, a veteran of the Pioneer Corps in World War Two, a Red Cross stalwart for over thirty years and the superintendent of the religious school for children attached to the main Tamil Hindu Temple. He was a steady and reliable man. He worked as a prisoner escort, taking men as far as Windhoek by train. One evening on his way home by train he was surrounded by six Blacks who slashed him up with knives before taking his firearm: nothing fatal, but about seventy stitches. By then he was about 68 and steadily lost his health, dying about eighteen months later. His funeral, under Tamil Hindu rites, unhappily rates as the most disorganised and disappointing I have ever been to, having no sense of ceremony or occasion.

Godfrey Hamshire was a large and jovial bloke, about 1,93m tall with an infectious laugh. He started as a junior engineer on Safmarine cargo boats, then came ashore to join a stevedoring firm in charge of cargo handling; and then followed his interest in computers into starting his own firm. He came from near Port Shepstone where he grew up speaking Zulu so well that he could pass himself off as one. He was promoted to sergeant and was well able to hold his own, working quite often with the detective branch.

Brigadier Eddie Kennedy was our district, then area, then provincial officer. I first met him when he was the Captain in charge of the Reserve Riot Unit. He had joined the Reserve soon after its formation in 1963 at Point when a teenager, and was one of the few members to have been awarded the long service medals for ten, twenty, and thirty years. He had been a commercial marine diver, the type who scrubs ships' bottoms or builds underwater pipelines, but then set up a security firm in Pinetown, running armed guards and rapid response teams. He was still fit and vigorous, keeping a tight ship. At the time of writing he was, after fifty years, the longest-serving member in the force.

Bernard Lancaster and his half-brother, Jan Snyders, were chalk and cheese. The first was fair and excitable; the other was black-haired, moustachioed and swarthy. Bernard loved to talk; Jan said little. Both had low-paid jobs but put in a fair bit of time and got their police work done, though one had to restrain Bernard's enthusiasm at times.

Denise McCormack was one of the first female reservists sworn in in Natal, and ten years later became one of the first female lieutenants in the reserve. She served at the Square until she moved to take command of the branch at Umbilo. She worked in insurance while bringing up her sons by herself. Entirely capable of quelling a crowd of wrestling fans or other excited types, being strongly built and strong-minded, she had, in many ways, to pioneer the way for our female members, both in how to deal with the public and with male members. I often used her to give lectures to recruits and older hands, both generally and for aspects of dress, uniform and deportment as they applied to our women.

Seggie Naidoo was a keen and effective member at the Square. He was a management trainee with Shell and doing well. After three years or so, he started to act rather out of character and seemed to be having unspecified difficulties both socially and at work. He resigned, cut contact with his friends and we suspected he had some mental health problems.

The brothers Iqbal and Yacoob Naroth both became sergeants at the Square. Iqbal was the more volatile one and was quite a lot shorter than Yacoob, who was some 1.88m tall. For some time Iqbal was considering taking a second wife, which as a Moslem he could do, which led to quite a bit of chaffing. As I recall, he gave up on that. Yacoob was one of, say, half a dozen members that I trusted to cover my back in a tight spot. At our braais, they and the other observant Moslems used to bring their meat wrapped in foil and cook it in the parcel, to avoid our pork-polluted foods. Mind you, they normally had marinated their stuff so we were entirely happy to share theirs.

Cravert Mnomiya was the best-performing Black member at Point. He was well-educated and spoke and wrote well in Zulu and English. He worked well despite a taxing domestic lifestyle, and bursts of whimsy.

Haresh Ragunath, generally known as Raggie, was one of the few members surviving from the old Central station, who became a sergeant at the Square. He was a driver for the Natal Blood Transfusion Service, and ran a small truck on the side, which he used to do a bit of house removals and other transport. Though quite short and slight he was no pushover, and was also one of the few I would choose to cover my back. His wife was a brilliant cook for breyani and samoosas. In passing, the best type of samoosa for the real enthusiast is the mashed potato, and hers were both crisp and tasty. Our braais were normally the best in the district.

An exotic among our officers was the district officer for Pinetown, with the rank of major, by name Alastair Upton. He was an old boy of Marlborough College in Wiltshire and had acquired the charming and dulcet tones of what we rustic colonials thought of as Brideshead English. He later moved down to Cape Town.

Nollie van Zyl came to Point as a sergeant from Pinetown and the Free State. He was also in insurance, a middle manager when with us, but after a couple of promotions left us to go upcountry. He was not tall, but solid and unflappable; the sort of bloke you could happily leave in charge of a duty and have no worries. The main problem simply was that his work absorbed more and more of his time.

Don Vermoter was one of our sergeants, first at the Square, then at Point. He was strong-minded but at times difficult, which was understandable given his service as an NCO in 41 Battalion in Angola. This was a unit drawn from the remnants of Holden Roberto's forces in the civil war, as opposed to Savimbi's who held the south for several years against the

Cubans and the communists. They were from the north and had a fearsome reputation as they had nothing to lose. They were set up as infantry with mainly South African officers and NCOs, though Angolans moved up through the ranks. Their colonel, curiously, was the poet Breyten Breytenbach's brother. Perhaps their most startling victory was against a brigade of infantry about three times their number, entrenched on one of the flat flood plains. The assault was made across 400 metres of plain with absolutely no cover, on foot, with no vehicles. They destroyed or drove off the entire brigade in about half an hour, for the loss of two men. Of course they had, the previous night, crept close to the enemy position and called out that they were 41 Battalion and they had come to this place to kill each one of their enemy. Don had then unwound for a couple of years on the Aberdeen oilfields.

John Walters was a long-serving member originally from Kent who, unusually, was married to a Lt-Commander in the SA Naval Reserve at SAS Nkonkoni. This, in passing, was the oldest volunteer reserve unit in the Royal Navy, with battle honours for the battle of Colenso. He came up through the ranks in the reserve platoon attached to the Reaction Unit. They reckoned they were the hard men, but our less charitable view was that they were more like vehicle guards and ammo waiters. He overcame this to become the number two at the Square, and once made up to lieutenant became branch commander. In his work he was a transport manager. His career was cut short by his early death from a stroke.

Tussie was a definite but generally well-liked character in and around Point. He lived in a Coloured suburb way out past Pinetown. He was a party animal with a lateral sense of humour and an impressive arrest record. In his twenties he was one of the few regulars who often came as a guest to the reservist parties or outings, where he generally was one of the cane-and-heavy-metal group. He was a good if not always orthodox cop.

His reward was to be shot down on the pavement, about 300 metres from the station. His killer emptied his revolver into him, which was a bad mistake as the bystanders promptly beat him to death. That was a pity, as there was no proof of who had hired him. This would have been very interesting as he turned out to have been a serving Indian SAP regular from Chatsworth.

One of our best female recruits was at Berea. She was a conscientious Scots girl from Elgin. I remember once in a house penetration exercise scaring her rigid. She was coming in; I was defending. As she spun into a doorway, pistol in hand, she found herself looking straight down my pistol barrel, about three inches in front of her eyes. The firearms were not loaded but …

However, their family home was broken into by two men while her mother was there; they raped her, which meant a real risk of infection with HIV/Aids. No formal complaint was made, but the whole family was back in Scotland within weeks.

At one time there was a reservist at Umlazi known as Dangerous Weapon. He was huge, about 2,02m tall, with arms so long there was no uniform shirt that could fit him, and police sizes went to *really* large. I once was issued a Warrant Officer's Sam Brown that came to below my hips. He was highly visible marching in his platoon with his sleeves rolled up half way and half a pace late on every movement. On the plus side he was a one-man road block.

Also at Umlazi was a regular with a trick that for years none of the magistrates believed. He would go into a cell carrying a bucket. Then he spoke to the prisoner, showing him his name tag: "I am Sergeant X. I am going to stand on this bucket and beat you up." And he did just that. How, I do not know.

At Point before my time there was an artful, chatty reservist, well known as the only guy in town who could go to a reservist camp with no money, drink there to his capacity, avoid gambling, but come back with cash in his pocket.

Some of the People

One of the more vivid characters who gave us weapons instruction in my early years was a Warrant Officer from the Reaction Unit called Tommy Stewart. He was not tall, but was wiry, agile and very fast. He could strip any weapon in about four seconds and reassemble it in six. That means the pieces come off so fast that one cannot reach the ground before the next is on its way. He remarked that you get that fast if you're doing it to clear a blockage under enemy fire. The demolition of trees with cortex, and throwing hand grenades over a hundred metres were his party pieces. He'd been in Rhodesia with the early SAP combat companies in about 1970, helping to fight the ZANU and ZAPU terrorists/guerrillas. He said the bloodiness of war first really struck him when he tried to recover the body of a friend blown up by a landmine, and couldn't fill an orange pocket with the remaining body parts. A pocket would be filled by less than two legs.

Another favourite with us was a big calm D/W/O called Faan vd Merwe. He first was a member of the Murder and Robbery squad, which was quite exciting, then joined the Bomb Disposal squad. After a couple of years there at the height of the terror bombings, he decided he'd better stop or die rapidly of lung cancer as he chain-smoked at bomb scenes. So he transferred to the photographic unit. Defusing was commonly done with a jet of water propelled by an explosion into the detonation gear, as that had to be disabled inside one-fiftieth of a second to beat the time of an AC electrical pulse. He thanked God the ANC never got round to using gas bombs.

One of our more unusual station commanders at Point was Capt Ian McCall. He had been in the Dog Squad so he had a couple of really big splendid Alsatians. His party trick was to play the bagpipes, which he did pretty well, though his occasional serenades around the station tended to disconcert the neighbours.

Chapter 4

STREETSWEEPING

The vast bulk of our work was done in the streets and other public places, sometimes in uniform, sometimes in plain-clothes. I believe the original idea was for Reserve members to work only in uniform in the company of and assisting regular members. This did happen to a greater or lesser extent in small rural stations, where reserve numbers were very small, but not in the bigger urban stations. Here there could often be twenty to fifty, and occasionally as many as three hundred, so the regulars were entirely happy to let us manage ourselves. We never really tried to have members working every day of the week, but focused on Fridays, Saturdays and public holidays, which tended to be the busiest. One reason for our concentration on plain-clothes work was the inefficiency of the uniform supplies, which came only from the Quartermaster in Pretoria, after a tedious and complex paperchase. As a result, a member would be lucky to get a full set of any uniform in his first year. The other reason was simply that it suited the type of work we did, which relied on being unobtrusive in the crowds in the centre of a large city.

We never worked alone. Vehicle crews consisted of a driver and a crew who handled the radio. Foot patrols could be as large as twelve, but then we would generally split into groups of two to four to operate within an area, sometimes in sight of each other. Uniformed members, if any, would pair off together, while plain-clothes people would be put together in reasonably credible groups, so they would not look odd. We did not go in for disguise but dressed in line with our age and style, simply so we did not stand out. To make sure that our pistols, handcuffs and other gear was not too visible we generally wore some sort of light jacket or long shirt over the holster. I commonly wore a light canvas zip-up jacket with a short-sleeved shirt and slacks. Though tourists did not spot us, the local street people could. Who else walks steadily, chatting but not looking at each other? We were even visible off duty, as you tend to develop a distinctive way of looking at people. I remember once in plain-clothes being announced by the whistling of the local drug dealers, a real midnight dawn chorus. Each group would have an NCO or experienced constable in charge, and ideally had a radio. Wherever possible they would be supported by a vehicle. The areas to be patrolled would be decided at the start of the shift, and rendezvous places and times fixed, normally with a fall-back time a half hour later for any group who could not make the original time. There are few things so irritating as having to search a city centre at 3am for missing members, which involves checking doorways and stairwells and turning over cartons and rubbish, when your concern is that they may have been stabbed or shot. Foot patrols were in practice only possible in central urban areas. Point's area of about six square kilometres allowed us to operate without a vehicle, save perhaps for the collection of people arrested; but at the Square, which covered at least twice the size, without a vehicle we were effectively limited to the beachfront. Visible policing or crowd control was always a uniform job, but we often had plain-clothes members follow the uniforms to watch the people who watched the uniforms.

We always, in the later years, were armed. In fact, I simply did not allow anyone outside the Charge Office without a pistol, while every vehicle carried a rifle, shotgun or HMC. There was a brief period after I became a lieutenant in 1990 when I merely carried a swagger stick, though my backup man was armed, but officers were soon instructed to wear a sidearm at all times, which made the swagger stick redundant. We also no longer got a sword, which rather disappointed John Walters and me, as we thought we'd look rather dashing rounding up evildoers at swordpoint.

Tear gas in the form of aerosol cans was issued personally to NCOs and senior constables. This could be very useful in ending fights, but had to be used with care in the open, not in a confined space. In extreme cases it could cause heart fibrillations and death, but could make an asthmatic pretty sick. We all had to undergo gassing in our basic training on range days so we knew what we were doing to others. In practice you nearly always got a waft of it when you sprayed it so we used it sparingly. Short wooden batons were issued in the early days but later tonfas came in for those trained on them.

Our independent shifts generally ran from, say, 6pm to midnight on a Friday and Saturday, with a day shift from, say, 8am to 6pm on Saturdays. Take-overs obviously had to coincide with regulars' shifts of 7 to 2, 2 to 9, and 9 to 7, or at times 12-hour 7 to 7 shifts. If we were busy, we often overran till dawn, and I can remember once or twice working as long as 17 hours, though this is not a good idea as you become increasingly error-prone. The real problem was that a Friday night 12-hour shift came on top of your normal working day, so, barring a couple of meal breaks, you might be active for 24 hours – definitely a young man's game.

However, for a flavour of our activities:

Chuck-out time at a posh pub. Husband and wife pause on the top step to enjoy the last of the air conditioning, and because at the foot of the stairs there were two of us in uniform.

"Good evening sir, good evening madam. Which of you is driving home?"

"I am," says she, taking the car keys from him very very fast.

"Oh good; have a pleasant drive."

Same place, another night, but several people on the steps.

"Good evening. Do any of you wish to commit an offence?"

Puzzled silence.

Hopefully: "Surely one of you wants to commit? Please won't someone commit even a tiny offence?"

More silence, then whispered discussions while keys changed hands.

*

Another good line, if you wanted to get the public to pay attention, was to say in proper deferential Jeeves style, "Can we assist you to the ground?"

*

It was three on a Saturday afternoon, a dead time in the central business district. It was warm and sunny. The early shift at the nightclubs was still to come out. We were drifting along in the van. I saw an agitated crowd of fifty or more people up ahead. As we neared I saw a City Policeman had made an arrest and was being pushed back by the crowd, who were protesting and shouting. We stopped and quietly climbed out and stood, side by side in the road. We were both in the heavy twill blue safari jackets and longs, Sam Browne, side arms, peaked cap and all. So far we had not been noticed. I put my right fist into my left hand in front of my chest, smiled and enquired, "Does anyone have a problem?" There was a pause. The crowd thought a bit, then dispersed. In forty seconds there were only the City Policeman, the arrestee and his brother.

*

The beachfront at night, a Coloured guy lying on the pavement surrounded by his pals: he's unconscious. He'd been drinking but his pals say he's a diabetic. Oh oh.

The paramedics come, attach a saline drip and give the bag to my sergeant Denise McCormack to hold up. The man revives, looks around puzzledly, registers the drip. "I'm OK, what is this shit? Take it off."

He starts to try to tear off the surgical tape, watched by an interested small crowd. At first we try to stop him, but the paramedics say, if he refuses treatment, that's it.

I look at him and say, "You realise it's unlucky to die on a Saturday?"

"Unnh ... why Saturday?"

"Isn't it obvious? Plus to which if you die I'll arrest you for littering and if you don't shift yourself I'll also do you for failing to remove litter."

At this Denise started laughing, followed a bit uncertainly by the crowd.

His pals got a car and took him home.

*

Another Saturday afternoon, in the complaints van with Denise. Radio Control calls us. Can we handle a disturbance at the Four Seasons Hotel? "Disturbance" was a very vague term, stretching from a singing drunk, to a gang fight with pangas, so we asked for more details. "Oh there are about fifty Hell's Angels causing a problem on the veranda." We look at each other: this could be interesting. I tell her, "Be ready to call for back-up."

The veranda bar was reached by a wide shallow staircase from the street. Parking was tight, so I drove our jolly yellow van up the stairs, parking on the top half and on the veranda. The Hell's Angels were there, but more like a hundred, sitting or standing around loose steel tables and chairs. I climbed out and walked onto the veranda closely followed by Denise, radio in hand. I stopped. We all looked in silence and with interest at each other for a few moments. I then asked for a manager. A junior one emerged quickly.

"Have you got a problem?"

"No, not really ..."

"Good."

" ... except for this guy ..."

This guy had a .357 Magnum revolver loaded with soft nose rounds which he had been spinning with his finger through the trigger guard in the middle of the bar. A real cowboy.

The Angels were happy. For the rest of our shift they waved and greeted us wherever we met. We felt like royalty.

*

It was the end of July Day at Greyville racecourse. We were clearing the bar areas in the Gold Ring so they could be closed. Punters liked to celebrate longer than the bar staff. Upstairs, there was a group of about six jovial Coloureds in their thirties, who had clearly had a couple of good wins they were still toasting. They were resistant to our charm and suasion, till I grabbed the main objector by his waist and right hand and waltzed him to the door amid the hoots of his friends.

*

A holiday Saturday night in my early days. My colleague, Steve, and I, in uniform, were making ourselves highly visible in the pubs and clubs area. A group of English speakers approached to ask for information. Their spokesman launched into his best, but dreadful, Afrikaans, hesitating and being prompted by his followers. We smiled encouragingly. Finally he stammered to a halt. My colleague replied, "I'm sorry sir," in his broadest Hampshire Hog accent. "I can't understand a word you said."

*

A disturbance at the Himalaya Hotel in the mid afternoon. I arrive with Sgt Chetty and Cst Iqbal Naroth. There we find an Indian man in his thirties orating and gyrating. The hotel management asks us to remove him. He seems to be mad or on drugs. We ask him nicely to come, but end up having to carry him twisting and kicking to the van where he tries to kick out the steel side grills and door. A cousin tells us he's an outpatient at Addington and has probably skipped his medication: so off to Casualty. There the duty nurse takes one look at him and asks us to stay, as the last time he came in, he smashed all the glass partitions and windows. She calls up his record and the duty doctor. Our patient was now peaceful, but telling us about his close personal friendships with the prime minister and other leading lights. We too were peaceful, standing around him with our batons drawn but behind our backs. A couple of security guards had turned up, but were trying hard to be inconspicuous. After what seemed like a long time the doctor arrived, so we took our man towards an examination bed. He promptly jumped up onto a windowsill and started to smash his way out of the window. Chetty reached up and plucked him down by his belt onto the bed, where we cuffed him. He was fighting and writhing, as he was a man possessed. Finally, he was secured to the bed by two leather restraint belts and two or three twisted sheets, but five of us were battling to hold him steady for a sedative injection. Then the doctor scoops a dozen or so varied needles out of his coat pocket – and starts wondering which to use.

*

The Himalaya Hotel seldom called us in for problems at their Black bars. If someone was daft or drunk enough to be a nuisance he would be taken outside by their securities. Four would surround him, two with knobkerries, two with sjamboks. They would work him over from head to knee, then handcuff him to a pole in the back courtyard. Last they would get a bucket of ice cubes and pour those down the front of his underpants. I never heard that one laid a formal complaint.

*

We once arrested a truck driver for abduction in the Himalaya and brought him and a fifteen-year-old girl from a room in it to the Square. It soon appeared he'd been smoking dagga in the room, so I sent Raggie back to search it. In the twenty minutes since the arrest the room had been cleaned and rented out to another couple. After the trial – where to the intense disgust of her parents, the infatuated girl's evidence was so bad the case collapsed – I told him he should give up on the dagga. He drove trucks on 600km trips to and from Jo'burg. He agreed, as he found if he smoked it he couldn't, at night, see oncoming headlights till they were twenty metres away.

*

One night, a couple of our regulars came on an armed robbery in progress at a beachfront restaurant. In the shoot-out, they killed two of the three robbers and wounded the third. One of our guys, though, took a bullet on the left cheekbone. The round broke into three bits which ricocheted up through his eye and brain and stopped at his skull. He lost the eye of course, but he was very lucky as, though his other injury was like a stroke, we could understand his speech after only two days. His daughter was too young to know what exactly had happened but his wife did.

And the restaurant owners? A husband and wife in their thirties, they had just renovated the place. One bullet smashed the main water pipe which flooded the restaurant. All the carpets and banquettes were ruined but the insurers refused to pay. They were not wounded but finished financially. They and their whole family left the country within two months.

*

One evening the opera was robbed. Two Black males held up the box office at gunpoint, seizing the night's takings. Our van was nearby so Radio gave us and others their descriptions. We spread out and started searching. Gun in hand we checked the bayside parks, the railway and bay shoreline and the underpasses under the railway – a good place to be able to shoot left-handed. We drew a blank, though we broke up a couple of romantic evenings. We fell back on the Opera House to regroup. As we came up the stairs in plain-clothes, with our firearms not in full sight but under jackets, I could see to the left the box-office staff, still wide-eyed; and to the right the foyer full of the interval crowd around the grand piano, nibbling num-nums and sipping drinkie-poos. Some were clearly wondering, "Who *are* these dreadful rough people? They're not even properly *dressed*."

One of the robbers was arrested in minutes, the other later.

*

New Year's Eve was always a major beachfront event, with perhaps 250 000 people on or near the beach. The roads within a block of the beach were closed to traffic and were chock-a-block with a complete mixture of people. One of us had acquired a bottle of champagne. As midnight struck, five of us were sharing it around the bonnet of our van in the middle of the crowd. Suddenly there was the sound of a shotgun blast near us. I dropped behind the engine. The guy opposite me came over the bonnet in a standing vault to land beside me, glass in hand. We unclipped our holsters and drew our pistols. After a bit, we worked out that there was a new firework in town that made the exact same sound, being tossed down from the tenth floor. So we finished the champers, of which remarkably little had been spilt.

*

Another big crowd-control job we had was the first visit of Nelson Mandela to Durban. He addressed a big rally at Kings Park, the rugby stadium. There was a big procession of political party activists in busloads from all sorts of places. This I watched in company with a group of regular Black NCOs, all of us sceptically observing the enthusiasm. We reckoned the sun would still rise in the east the next day, and we would be fighting the same criminals. The most ironical banner I saw was that of the Delville Wood Young Comrades Branch of the Communist Party. Delville Wood was a railway halt named for the WW1 battle in France where a SA infantry brigade had gone in, some 3 000 strong. After three days repelling German attacks, about 350 survivors marched out. It was the SA equivalent of the Somme.

*

One of the seeming conventions of English detective fiction is that people see a corpse and throw up. This is complete rubbish. It simply doesn't happen. Rather cover the corpse if it is in a street, and charge passers-by a fee to lift the covering off the face. You'll make a small fortune.

*

If you want to look really cool when you arrive at a scene, slide in forwards with the handbrake on. Just before the car stops, you jump out of the driver's door with your firearm in your right hand. As the car carries through, use your left hand to open the back door to release the dog. This gets you in play before the car stops, very useful in a fire fight. This was a trick of Ian McCall and some of the Dog Squad.

*

Car chases by our vehicles? You have got to be joking. Anything over 80kph and we started cheering or screaming, depending. I once had the accelerator pedal fall off at that speed. My crew had to dive to retrieve it before it jammed the brake. Another time with 14 prisoners in the back we nearly grounded the rear and I could only steer to within 20 degrees, rather like aquaplaning. In passing, the vans had a steel back portion roofed and with grills along the sides above the steel benches which could take four a side. To get 14 in you slid the last two in horizontally on the laps of those sitting on the floor or benches.

*

Perhaps the fastest chase I ever did was from the Blue Swan cafe in the CBD to the Umgeni River. We were looking into reports of robbery on the late buses to Phoenix. Three of our plain-clothes Indian and Coloured members, including Seggie Naidoo and Roy Pietersen, got on the last bus. Three more of us in uniform followed in a van. To our surprise, the bus took off at over 100kph in a 60 limit, straight up Umgeni Rd, taking a couple of lights on the amber. Going flat out, nearly taking off on the bumps, I only managed to catch up on the Umgeni River bridge, about 5kms north.

*

The classic non-Keystone chase took place in my early days. I was crewing late at night, basically acting as a guide, with two members from Durban North in for a joint operation, driving their Landrover. Their senior man was a minister, his driver an undertaker. We had an urgent call to a double stabbing about a block away from us, in the front of the old Tech building. The shortest route would have been the wrong way up a four-lane one-way, about 150m in all. I suggested that. No, we drove at hearse speed down the block following the one ways, stopping at empty pedestrian crossing lights, both down and back, plus the main lights. By the time we arrived one man was dead, the other near death, both stabbed in the groin.

*

Thefts of, or out of, motor vehicles were a perennial problem. Generally the theft could only be proved by an eye witness. Failing that, you might be able to charge for possession of stolen property from the vehicle or of a key, possibly cut down to make a master, or of tampering with a motor vehicle. The rough types might use a rock on a side window, the more sophisticated a wire through the window trim to hook the release button, or a tennis ball and a brick, before hotwiring the car. I have known a car stolen in under a minute without the people in the car parked right behind it realising it was a theft. Most cars were stolen to order, and dismantled or resprayed and new engine and chassis numbers put on by chop shops. Expensive cars like Mercedes were often exported to other parts of Africa, or even Brazil or Australia. I had a client who found his posh nearly new Landrover had been stolen in Belgium. One theft did amuse most of us. A local restauranteur was first to buy the newest theft-proof electronically keyed Merc, and this even featured in the local paper. Three days later it was stolen. It turned out the salesman who gave him the two keys had forgotten to mention the third.

I was therefore charmed to discover an old Natal statute, one of the last passed before Union in 1910, which created an offence of deemed housebreaking when someone was found in possession of housebreaking tools. I checked that it was still in force. It was.

Soon after I was on foot with Iqbal Naroth and Seggie Naidoo one evening, when someone phoned in from an Esplanade flat to say a couple of men were trying the handles of cars parked there, and were turning towards the Workshop. We stepped out from the corner, stopped and searched them. We found a knife and a screwdriver, so to their surprise we arrested them for housebreaking. At court I first had to persuade the prosecutor that the charge was possible. As this only applied to Natal, justice training in Pretoria knew nothing of it. He then put the charge, at which the magistrate adjourned so he could check it was valid. I then gave detailed evidence on the facts of the tools, which were exhibits. The knife blade was blunt and scuffed extensively on the sides by being shoved through metal window frames, while the star screwdriver was too worn to turn a screw, and was bent slightly in a couple of places from being used as a lever. They both got three months. I then passed on the good news to the regulars and reservists generally.

*

When patrolling in a vehicle we seldom went fast. Unless speed was necessary we would normally tick along at about 20kph so we could watch exactly what was going on. One night there were four of us in a car when Radio sent us to an armed robbery in progress in Stamford Hill. We stopped, turned off the headlights to improve our night vision, discussed how we should approach the scene, cocked our five weapons, opened all the doors a little, then drifted quietly to the shop. The sound of the cocking makes a distinct impression as a prelude to action. The doors were opened so we could roll out very fast if we came under fire. That one turned out to be an anti-climax, a possible abduction for rape and murder which had us searching the local cemetery in the pitch dark.

*

Only once did one of my members have to shoot anyone. Some man was trying to chop Sgt Chetty's head off with a panga so he shot him in the chest. There was a puzzled pause. Chetty thought he'd be knocked over, but he wasn't. He didn't really believe he'd been shot. Only when he felt the blood pouring down his back did he sit down.

*

I only once was involved in a case of police brutality. I was at work down at our Amanzimtoti office when two black men turned up to complain that they had been beaten by the police at the local station. I got them to strip off their shirts and saw they had been flogged. As they could not speak much English, I got a friendly Zulu from a neighbouring office to translate, then had a set of photos taken by the local photographer, who had agreed to be a witness in court if needed. Both had been hit with a cane, one about fifteen times, the other half that, after being "arrested" but never formally charged with anything by two young white constables, and taken to an office at the station. I took statements, then gave the case to my litigation partner who sued and got them about R3 000 and R1 700 each, at a time when they could have earned as labourers about R200 per week. This result greatly cheered my colleagues in the Reserve, as this type of behaviour really annoyed us.

*

If you want to see someone stop dead from a sprint in mid-air, try shouting "Stop!" … while you cock your shotgun.

*

Nicknames for the police apart from the usual English terms included:

- *dienaars* as in *"die dienaars is met ons"*, an old Cape warning; from *geregsdienaars*, a term used, I believe, for the old Cape Town watchmen before 1850,
- *langarms*, also from the Cape, where it could refer equally to police, the long arm of the law, or baboons, and
- various graphic Zulu words, one of which means the thin green stool produced when you have dysentery.

*

Sgt Nollie van Zyl and I were patrolling one night, with a new recruit, Ben Lenz, watching how it was done. A Black man flagged us down, bleeding from a dozen or so minor stab wounds on his face, neck, shoulders and chest. He explained he had been stabbed by another Black male acting strangely in a block of flats on Rutherford Street. We took him along to point this man out. The block was deserted with the power turned off. Nollie and I looked at each other, drew and cocked our pistols, and went up the stairs by torchlight. On the third-floor landing we found two Blacks, one wide-eyed and bleeding in places, the other glassy eyed with a knife in hand. The only light was from a candle in a saucer on the floor. We were still on the stairs. Nollie and I immediately took aim. The other two tried to get under the wallpaper. Nollie shouted at him in English and Zulu to put the knife down. He turned to us and started to walk forward. He seemed drunk, drugged or insane, certainly unpredictable. He got to about two paces from Nollie, then very slowly stopped and put down the knife. We charged, flattened and cuffed him.

Comparing notes afterwards, it turned out that, had he taken one more step, we would both have shot him dead; two rounds from Nollie to the heart, two from me to the head.

*

One practical problem we had to solve was, how do two of you collect and move people who are either inert or uncooperative? Men generally are easier as they wear belts. If you hoist one by the belt at the small of the back, one – or if he is big, two – of you can carry him like a suitcase. OK, his hands and feet may drag a bit, but so? Women's clothing in the sub-tropics was too light to be useful, and would most likely tear or pull off.

Raggie had a useful trick to deal with the upright but awkward. He called us one night, saying he was about to arrest two Black males on his own, could we drive round to collect?

We drove there fast, but found him standing peaceably with two large guys lying at his feet cuffed together and moaning. I raised an eyebrow. "Oh I just lifted them by the belt and as they fell forward drove their heads into the tarmac."

*

One hot night Raggie and I had arrested a grimy female, and brought her in a truck to the Square. When we opened the back, we found her still drunk, fat and sweaty, but now also naked. We managed to get her out the truck but she lay on the tarmac, wailed and refused to get dressed. We tried to manhandle her, but couldn't get any grip on her at all. Neither of us particularly wanted her rubbing against our uniforms. Raggie went inside to get help. He returned with a female regular. She looked at the woman, and told her to get dressed and come. She carried on wailing, so our lady pulled out her teargas canister and gave her a long steady spray from neck to groin, paused there and went up again. Teargas stings like crazy on wet skin. "*Woza,*" she repeated, and this time the naked woman trotted briskly inside.

*

Another very awkward female Godfrey and I met one night when a sad, small man came to Point to say his ex-girlfriend was sitting in his flat and refusing to leave: could we help? He was the tenant. His problem was obvious once we got into the bedroom. The friend was scarcely 1,60m tall but weighed about 150kg. We tried persuading her to go, but she remained an abject, weeping mass on the bed. Her arms were so fat that we could get no grip on them, and the fat swung around the bones of her upper arms. Finally we managed by sliding our arm to the elbow under her armpit, grabbing her elbow with our other hand, then hoisting her by brute force and carrying her out the flat. That though was not simple, as we had to negotiate six large aquaria of tropical fish in a small living room. He bolted, locked and chained the door the moment we were out. As she refused to get in the lift, we finally left her sitting in the rain next the stairs.

*

The best way to seize someone you're detaining or arresting is for two of you to grip the upper arm at the armpit and the arm just above the elbow, and to hoist him off or nearly off his feet, then walk him away. He has great difficulty trying to kick or bite you. Trying to hold a leg is difficult and quite dangerous, given that the leg muscles are the strongest in the body. In passing, one thing you should never do is to lean over someone lying down and shake their shoulder, or touch their face, unless you fancy being strangled or having a finger bitten off. A swift kick to the arch of the foot is a good test of someone's condition, and leaves you well out of range of an attack.

We normally handcuffed people behind their back. That way they cannot club you or garrotte you with the cuffs, nor can they run fast without falling, and if necessary you can control them with one finger. If we had to cuff two people with one pair of cuffs, we cuffed their right wrists together, so they would find it hard to run. One thing we never dreamed of doing was handcuffing ourselves to a prisoner. Nor would we ever put a prisoner behind the driver of a car.

*

We arrested people if we could charge them, a so-called straight charge, if we had ourselves seen them commit the offence. If we were not eye witnesses but relied on witnesses, then initially we detained them as suspects, and could hold them for up to 48 hours as such. To ensure that there was no ambiguity about what we were doing, we had to tell them that they were being arrested, or detained, as the case might be, and for which offence, and then caution them. We also had to put a hand on their shoulder while doing that, or as the law rather coyly permitted, confine their body. Even using the minimum necessary force, this sometimes needed four or six policemen to seize and subdue one man sufficiently to get him into a van or cell. On the other hand, I once while on my own arrested three men simply by calling out to them across the road, but they were admittedly all drunk.

*

Incidents with women did at times have their own strange character. One day while on complaints, we were called to a shoplifting at a fashionable clothing store. On arrival, we were greeted by a solid wall of screams coming from the changing booth. The rather shattered manageress told us they had put the shop lifter in there, after she had, when challenged, sprayed breast milk over the till and started shouting, all in an effort to embarrass her way out. When I whipped open the curtain and said "Yes?" she shut up. She turned out to be an old hand with a dozen or more convictions.

Another shoplifter I arrested had lifted a dozen blouses still on their steel hangers, and hidden them between her thighs. When I asked the female store detective where she had put the hooks, I got a very strange look. One I heard of concerned a stout lady who was in a long queue at the tills. When others noticed her standing in a pool of blood-streaked water, they rushed to get help thinking her waters had broken, but it turned out to be three frozen chickens.

Another unusual one concerned a woman trying to steal a purse tucked under the seat of a pushchair a toddler was sitting in. The mother, who had been looking at a display, fortunately turned in time to grab the purse back. The thief immediately claimed she was trying to save it from falling on the floor. Luckily the victim, who had been considerably shaken by the incident, lived nearby, so we took her home and got her to explain why the thief was lying. This needed her to act out the whole series of movements made by them both, so I wrote her statement pretty much like a choreography. Again the thief was an old offender and was jailed for over two years.

The most persistent thief was an old woman I once arrested for possession of stolen property, in her case several bed sheets. Her first conviction was in pounds shillings and pence, before decimalisation in 1961.

*

Four of us were taking a coffee break at the Excel. Radio Control gave us two complaints: one the eviction of an unwanted lodger, the other dagga being smoked on the roof of a block of flats: neither very exciting. After a bit of a chat we took the dagga, the regulars the lodger. We found evidence of smoking but no smokers. When the lodger was told he must go as his ex-friend was the tenant, he slipped past the friend through the living room across the balcony and out off the third floor. The impact sheared both legs off just above the knees. He died after 40 minutes.

*

It was dawn on a Sunday. We were winding down the night shift on a take-over at the Square. A rather drunk guy wandered in looking a bit shattered.

"Good morning sir. What can we do for you?"

"Well it's this pal of mine: he seems to have disappeared."

"Seems?"

"Well, he was at my place last night but he hasn't got home."

"OK, let's get some details." So we took notes of names, addresses, and such like. He lived in a flat on the twelfth floor of a block at the bottom of Innes Rd.

"Ja, well we were all pretty trashed at about one this morning when Andre said he must be going, so he got up, went to the door, opened the window and stepped out. At least I think I saw that, but hey." At which he burped, nearly passed out, but half fell onto a bench, still really *babbelaas*. Normally we noted statements by drunks but did not often act on them, the fruit

Streetsweeping

of hard experience. This was however pretty weird so I sent a van to the flat. They had a look around. Andre had indeed stepped out the window and landed in the drying yard at ground level. He was very dead. We told his friend, who sobered enough that we didn't have to arrest him.

*

If we needed urgent backup, the drill was to cut into the normal radio traffic with a shout of "Break, break, break!" Then obviously you gave your location and details of your problem. The results could be fairly spectacular. The first van to arrive to one call slid sideways into the edge of the crowd after ninety seconds. Four others got there inside five minutes.

Three of us were on a traffic island on the corner of Rutherford and Point Road dealing with an incident where a gang of Black males had snatched a heavy solid gold Buddhist medallion from the neck of a Japanese lady. Her companions had fired shots, grabbed the thief and recovered the medallion, but were swiftly surrounded by a crowd of Blacks. By the time we got there, there were, say, 70, which very soon doubled. They were crowding us and the Japanese. If you assume, as we did, that every man there was carrying a six-inch blade, this was a potentially fatal situation. For good measure, you'd be very fortunate to catch any knifeman in such a crowd.

One lucky touch to this was that one bullet fired in the air went through a second-floor window. The little old man who usually sat at that window had just gone to the loo.

*

Apart from the knives and the occasional commercially made firearm, another weapon we were always alert for was the so-called homemade. I was once acting as the orderly at a Small Claims Court when a Black woman came to get her money back on a defective revolver made in KwaMashu. It had five chambers, each with a different type of round in it. She won her damages, but I referred the case to the firearms squad. More simple, and more common, was the one-shot handgun made from an angled piece of wood, a nail, a spring, a form of trigger and a length of pipe into which a shotgun round had been fixed. If it did not blow its owner's hand off when he ran right up to his victim, it would almost certainly kill. To some extent, this replaced the assegai in rural faction fights, and raised the death rate. It cost roughly the equivalent of five loaves of bread.

*

The other time I called for backup was outside a stevedores' hostel in Congella. My crew and I were taking someone to King Edward VIII hospital, when an urgent radio call came through to attend a traffic incident with injuries right outside the hostel entrance. We were a block away so we took it. This hostel was a large four-storey building that housed several hundred contract labourers. The police never entered it, save in squads of sixteen all armed with shotguns or automatic weapons, as it was a fair assumption that there would be at least one AK47 and several handguns plus spears, knobkerries and knives in the rooms, and plenty of strong guys happy to use them.

On arrival I found a docker had been run down, breaking both legs. He had just been taken to hospital. The driver, though, was still sitting in his car in the middle of a four-lane road. He was a senior Black patrolman with the City Police. His blood alcohol content later proved to be 0.30, nearly four times the limit. I was astonished to find three City Policemen there, who had not arrested or protected him from the 150 or so dockers who were swarming close around and between them and the driver. This time I called specifically for two Dog Units, plus anyone else. While we waited for them, we put the driver in the back of our van, and locked the door with a pair of handcuffs to discourage any revenge attack. I then started to measure the scene, walking from point to point through the crowd, and shooing them like cattle out of my way with swings of my arms and shouts of "Huut huut!". This surely must have seemed distinctly eccentric; but, importantly, it kept me the initiative. They were still wondering what this daft mlungu would do next rather than attacking me. We were joined first by four Riot Unit members, one of whom announced their arrival by smashing a pole-mounted rubbish bin with his tonfa stick. The dogs didn't need that sort of advertising.

*

Steve West and I were on complaints on the Saturday afternoon of the Currie Cup rugby final, when Radio sent us to a block of flats used as a temporary barracks by student constables from the Police College in Pretoria brought down to boost the riot units. He was then a security at Addington and one of our sergeants, but later joined the provincial traffic police.

It was a shooting. We went in, jumping over one student having a major fit, possibly epileptic, in the passageway. The scene was in a room. The dead man was nineteen, scarcely more than a boy. He lay on his back across a bed. Blood was dripping steadily from an entry wound in the left rear of his skull into a pool of blood on the parquet floor. He and his room-mate, who turned out to be the one having the fit, had been eating white bread and banana sandwiches and drinking brandy and ginger ale. A Z88 lay near his left hand on the bed. A *doppie* lay on the floor in front of and somewhat to his left. He still had a sandwich in his right hand. He was still bruising. A bullet in the back of the head gives a splendid pair of black eyes. The bruises carried on swelling for about forty minutes after his death. I spent the time making a detailed sketch of the scene and trying to stop senior officers disturbing the scene. The colonel of the Riot Unit, the duty officer, and the police chaplain among others were all there, trying to see if it was a suicide or not. Judging by the position of the pistol and the angle of the wound from left rear where I saw no scorch marks, to the right temple where the bullet had jammed in the skull; it was not. Plus to which, who shoots himself halfway through a sandwich? I never heard the inquest verdict.

*

Steve West was involved in another odd death, his mother's. She was a matron at a hospital in Zululand when she suddenly died. A stroke or cerebral haemorrhage was diagnosed. Steve went up to make the formal identification of the body. He noticed that that the inside corner of her left eye was discoloured like a bruise. He called attention to it, an X-ray was done, and a .22 bullet found in her head. Her boyfriend was later arrested.

*

The nightclubs shut at 4am, while the sun rose between 5:30 and 6:30, so you got a weird mixture of their clients and early surfers, the guys who went before going to work. On the one hand, hung-over black-clad Goths or cockroaches trailing around; on the other, keen, lively and ebullient athletes. The spaced-out surfers arrived much later.

One dawn, we came on two overdressed and disarrayed females standing each side of a tomato box upended in the middle of the street, sloshing each other with their handbags, while their beaus cheered them on. They only stopped when they heard us laughing.

*

330 was a busy and popular night club in Point Road. It held regular fancy dress nights which raised some practical problems: for example, is a pantomime horse one arrest or two? These and other dark matters occupied our philosophical energies in the night shifts.

We would have loved to have taken the drug sniffer dogs

into 330 but the place was too crowded for them to be effective, as it was a warren of small rooms that had been offices or storerooms, spread over three floors.

Their parking lot was a regular port of call. In it was a fairly tall tree. Once we kicked the tree and a guy smoking zol fell nearly twenty feet out of it. Another effective business method was to order your shotgun man to clear the tree, let him cock it – the sound is surprisingly loud – and wait a bit.

*

There were a lot of nightclubs in the Point area. Many changed hands, names and styles repeatedly, but some stayed the pace. Their character and clientele varied wildly. Some were White, some Indian, some Coloured, a couple mixed as they focused on sailors, one did jazz and transvestites, the odd one homosexuals, but none were Black. This continued after the racial laws fell away.

The noisiest was a short-lived heavy metal dump. There the sound waves hit your chest, a most disquieting sensation; if you stood still, you slowly drifted across the cement floor.

The most dangerous was a Coloured place with serious bouncers who removed all firearms and weaponry from guests. Still, there was a steady trickle of shootings and knifings in or near the place. We preferred only to enter in fours.

The safest was the Goth club at the new railway station.

The most stylish was a restored late-Victorian two-storied house which catered for gays and lesbians. I watched South Africa win the Rugby World Cup there, at the invitation of its owner.

*

Our normal line of attack on undesirable clubs was on their liquor sales, either because they breached their liquor licences or because they had no licence at all. If nothing else, our seizures of their stock wore them out financially.

One such, called Neptune's, was run by a spherical, bald lady, 1.6m tall and called TC, which she proudly told me was her father's name for her and stood for Terrible Child. He must have been far-sighted. We had this chat one night while most of Point moved seven vanloads of booze out of her unlicensed dive, even though she claimed to be looking after it for her son's twenty-first in Durban North. Her care was impressive: she had carefully put all the beers in large galvanised baths filled to the brim with ice. Her star attraction was a dancer who did things with a baseball bat that beat the Siamese ping-pong ball trick. Guys were coming from Mooi River and further to see and disbelieve.

*

A practical problem of noise in the clubs was that anyone coming out after a couple of hours had an increased level of aggression which could last for hours. Hence the fact that nearly all headbutting assaults took place outside nightclubs.

*

Hotels, on the whole, gave us very few problems. We only went into licensed premises by invitation of the licensee. A couple in rather out-of-the-way streets could be described as knocking shops, but they did at least try to be discreet. The one curious one in Point Road was the St. James, which was probably a survivor of the old hard-drinking establishments used by stokers and other muscular types. All its furniture was bolted down and there were no glasses, only plastic tumblers. One regular there had lost both forearms, and when drunk used to make lewd and crude suggestions while nudging you with his stumps. If he became too much of a nuisance, his pals would take off his wooden leg and leave him squirming on the floor.

*

A potentially very dangerous type was a steroid user in a

so-called "roid rage". Then they really are longing to hear bones break, and can indulge themselves rather effectively. Bear in mind that the steroids were taken to bulk up muscle tissue by bodybuilders or weightlifters, so they were unusually strong. It's easy to break an arm across a wall, and I've heard eyewitness accounts of legs being broken by being jumped on while across a gutter. In one case, the victim was thrown over a security fence to be finished off by a small pack of Rottweilers.

This problem grew markedly in the 1990s, when one of these roid types set up a security/bouncer outfit that found its opposition falling apart and clubs remarkably willing to hire them. As you can imagine, finding local and live witnesses became tricky.

The one upside was that users don't live long: they are prone to strokes or heart attacks.

*

Arguably the nearest I came to being beaten to a pulp was one night on the beachfront. John Baldock and I found three big guys, possibly a father and two sons, each over 1.90m tall and wide, built like weightlifters, all fighting drunk. The two youngsters were rolling to and fro on the raised side of a large decorative pond, grappling with and trying to strangle each other. They would not stop when asked so I gassed them both. At this, father, who had been encouraging the brawl, became upset and planted himself with his chest touching mine, threatening me with voice and fists. Baldock, standing about two paces to my right, was sufficiently concerned to cock his shotgun. I stood my ground and told father he would be making a grave error of judgement if he assaulted me. After a minute or two of debate, he calmed down a little and left with his two tearful boys.

On reflection, I am quite proud of the fact that in eighteen years' service I was never assaulted. This may not sound significant but to a policeman it is.

*

We were quite often asked if we were scared when on duty. As a rule, our answer was: "No we're too busy to be scared."

An illustration of this took place one evening at the then new Exhibition Centre. This had just opened, so I went in with a patrol to fly the flag and find out what went on. With me was Yacoob Naroth. We met the manager – funny how quickly uniformed police meet the boss – who was showing us around the complex, when someone rushed out of the disco saying there's a firearm incident. We look at the manager, think, "Oh shit," but say "That'll be for us," and run into the disco.

There the crowd of about 200 was backing off in all directions from a pair of men, one White, one Coloured, facing each other and shouting. Naroth and I pushed in between them, standing back to back. The White guy had no weapon, but the Coloured had a Colt 45. The muzzle was pressed against Naroth's chest. Had he fired, the bullet would have gone straight through Naroth, killing him – and me too most likely. Yacoob instantly pushed the weapon down and cuffed him while I very quickly but carefully grabbed the Colt, dropped out the magazine, found a round in the chamber, the weapon cocked and the safety catch off.

After the excitement was over, we looked at each other. I said, "That was a bit hairy."

He said "Yes."

We seized the weapon and started an enquiry into his fitness to possess a firearm.

*

I made a point of talking to the owners or operators of the cafes and shops on our beats. After all they spent their days watching the street and gossiping, so they could always tell us what was

Streetsweeping

going on. Regular visits made good PR, and produced lots of jokes whether in Greek, Portuguese Indian or other accents.

*

At the Square when I was a sergeant, I was part of a regular Saturday morning squad hunting bagsnatchers, snatch thieves, car thieves and such like in the CBD and Grey Street area. The *skotens*, a Zulu term for a bad bastard, would start to arrive at 9:00 to 9:15. By then my crew and I, in uniform, would be in an Indian furniture shop in Pine Street with a view right down Albert, sitting comfortably with the manager with cups of tea, looking out at the baddies coming towards us from the bus and taxi ranks. In passing, I always went in uniform, as any White in plain-clothes in the Grey Street area would be suspected of being a cop and certainly would stand out like a lighthouse. My snatch squads who'd had their tea took position in plain-clothes round the street corners, waiting our radio call or their own suspicions. The give-aways were a knife and a bag containing an extra T-shirt and cap. Unless they were wanted, their knives were seized, they were warned and sent home.

After that we generally went hunting. I would drive the plain-clothes squad to a point, drop them off, and give them, say, an hour to move through an area like the arcades in the Grey Street area, and then meet at another point to collect those they had arrested. Often they were cuffed to parking meters with one member to guard them. He then would travel back to the Square to do the paperwork. The commonest charge was theft by snatching. Indian women used to wear gold lockets on necklaces, though this had nearly died out as a result of the snatch thefts. The squad was so effective that when Seggie Naidoo was made up to sergeant, within two days the crooks were congratulating him, remarking that he should be thanking them.

A pretty effective form of crime prevention was used by the

regular crime prevention squad to reduce thefts on Saturdays. Late on a Friday afternoon, too late for them to get a bail hearing until Monday, they arrested all the fences who bought from street thieves, who then could not sell on their takings during the weekend, so they gave up, even at times dumping the goods

*

One day we came on a disturbance, lots of shouting, some pushing in front of an appreciative crowd. I sent a couple of my guys in to arrest one noisy Black man. He, outraged, shouts at me: "You're only doing this to me because I am a kaffir."

I simply replied: "No, I'm doing this to you because you are a cunt." That settled the matter and cheered the crowd.

*

One of the simplest but surprisingly effective con tricks was done in the arcades. The sucker would be shown a decoy example where a banknote is rolled in brown paper with certain *muti*; held tightly in the hand for two minutes while eyes are shut and a magic word repeated. Open the paper and there are two banknotes. Some people kept trying for ten minutes or more.

The three-thimble trick was done down on the beachfront to catch the tourist trade, generally by Blacks or Indians, sometimes using a White accomplice. The trick is to check the operator's fingernails. One at least is long.

At one point one-armed bandits, or slots, were becoming arguably legal, but there were some contradictory court cases. I looked in at a number of clubs around the beachfront to ask what percentage of the take was paid out in wins or jackpots. This is set inside each machine. The payouts ranged from 68 to 83%.

*

At Point I arranged the use at our discretion of the podium roof of a beachfront hotel, the Malibu, which gave us a brilliant view of half the beach and the gardens. We also used a ten-storey block's roof to photograph drug dealers watching them through a long lens. People never think to look up for surveillance even when they are very conscious of ground level. The regulars also used a beachfront flat for observation. A couple of restaurant owners, like the Portuguese brothers who ran the El Cacador, could identify individual *skotens*. If there was nothing else to do I'd send a couple of members to follow them closely till they gave up and left our area.

*

One place where I really had people clustering to watch me pass in uniform was the so-called European Market, as opposed to the Indian Market, where halaal and Hindu butchers and spice merchants among other exotica were centred. It struck me one day that I'd gone past it hundreds of times but never into it, so I went in and met the market master. He reckoned it was the first time in about nine years that a policeman had made a social call. Each market was a large covered building full of stalls. The stallholders were almost all Indian, the clientele was everyone but Europeans who were deterred by the crime in the area. I subsequently popped in from time to time for a cup of tea, if only to make it clear this was not a no-go area, something no police force can allow.

*

In one case, a bit before midday on a busy Saturday morning in Field St, at the entrance to the parking garage I personally used for work, an eleven-year-old Indian boy was standing waiting for his father to meet him. Three Coloured men strolled up to him, stood around him, drew long flick-knives, and for no obvious reason stabbed him eleven times through the body. He collapsed. They strolled off.

Sgt Chetty and I were doing a uniform foot patrol with four other members. We came on the scene just as he was loaded into the ambo. Eyewitnesses gave us reasonably good descriptions of all three. We followed their likely routes. I went to the Coloured bus and taxi ranks to check all passengers that could match the descriptions for blood spatter. Basically you stop each bus; one stays with the driver to stop him driving off and the other two go down the bus asking anyone vaguely resembling the suspects to stand up so you can see their clothes. All very polite, but your holster is unclipped and your hand on your pistol. We drew a blank, but Chetty and his pair who had headed towards Currie's Fountain found a derelict house with about twenty Coloureds and Blacks in it, drinking and smoking dagga. They went in and removed the three at gun point.

*

One morning at about 4:30, I drove into the deserted intersection of Alice Street and Argyle Road to find a dead Black man sprawled in the road. He had just been stabbed several times in the neck and shoulder and had bled to death. The sprays of blood from his neck wounds had left a clear spoor as he had staggered around, so we backtracked about 250m to where he had been stabbed. Nearby I located a Black night watchman from northern Natal who explained to me in Afrikaans that the dead man had been wandering drunkenly along singing as he went, when a group of four or more Indians aged about twenty had come along, met him, stabbed him, then walked towards Berea railway station. I sent a van down there, but they found no trace of them. The mortuary van arrived and covered the corpse while we waited to hand over the scene to someone from Murder and Robbery. The early morning stream of commuters started at five to five. They all wanted to see who it was, but when the face was that of a stranger they completely lost interest and resumed their conversations.

*

Streetsweeping

The back of the Kit-Kat Cafe was the scene of another stabbing. About 3:00 we found a Black man face down on the pavement, stabbed and apparently bled out. This gives a pool of blood about the size of an average desk, and about half a centimetre deep. His shoes had been stolen so we reckoned his killer was almost certainly another Black. While we waited for the mortuary van to arrive we noticed what seemed to be some slight movement of the body, so although neither of us thought it possible that he was not dead, we called an ambo to check him. They came and found he was in rigor and the movement must have been caused by his clenched hands relaxing a bit. We then flipped him over, and found he was like a tailor's dummy with some thirty or more wounds in the chest and stomach to add to the dozen or so in his back. As was commonly the case he had no ID.

In the meantime another Black man, who seemed a bit subnormal, wandered along stepping over the corpse's left leg, then his left arm, before we stopped and questioned him. It turned out he had been past at least once before, stepping over the body. He then asked if we were interested in dead people. We could be; but why? Oh, says he, there's another one down by the bridge. I sent a van down to the nearby pedestrian bridge from the railway station to the bus ranks where sure enough, they found another guy jammed head down between the bridge support and a toilet block. It seemed he'd been stabbed, robbed and tossed off the bridge.

*

To track a blood spray trail you have to get there pretty soon, certainly before there has been much foot or vehicle traffic. Fresh splashes are fairly obvious but as it dries it tends to blend into the general mess. If you shine a torch along the ground and look carefully down the beam, you see an effect like tiny red cats' eyes. In my early days, we even took a dab on a fingertip and tasted it, as blood tastes salty. Once Aids arrived that trick stopped. We all tried to carry a couple of sets of surgical gloves to prevent contamination, though that would not prevent needlestick injuries, which at first were a source of real worry. The trouble was that no-one was really sure how infectious or contagious it was, but we understood that a victim showed no positive signs of infection for six weeks after catching it, and that a lot of people, especially Blacks, had it. This was simply the result of a polygamous mindset and comparatively casual sexual habits. We simply assumed everyone had it and acted accordingly. Anecdotally we heard that up to 70% of the black workforce aged from 15 to 45 in some industries was infected. Certainly the Natal Blood Transfusion Service abandoned visits to factories and other large employers, and shifted its emphasis away from whole blood to plasma and other products.

*

The newspapers used to run a regular article listing off the murders of the previous day, generally on the lower half of page 2 or 3, often with the last half dozen being unknown Black males shot stabbed or beaten to death. Not infrequently if you counted you'd find they'd left off a couple, presumably to save space.

*

An area that routinely drew our attention at the Square was "the bridge", a piece of unpaved ground under the freeway flyover on the seaward side of the railway at Berea Road station, which gave access to the main pedestrian bridge over the tracks, and the Brooke Street mosque. As such it was a natural chokepoint, so that on a Saturday you could easily have hundreds of Blacks and Indians walking through four abreast for hours. The daily commuter throughput by rail and road was at least 250 000. The bridge served as an unofficial market and entertainment spot, with fruit and toothpaste – three for ten bob – the most common. Musicians were nearly always there, some, alas, with heavy speakers hooked up to car batteries, playing Black music idioms ranging from jazz to the style of Ladysmith Black Mambazo.

An unusual weightlifter used to lift a V8 engine with his teeth: he bit on a leather belt around a hoist chain padlocked to the engine. Some years later, I found him in semi-retirement acting as a doorman at a central hotel. I asked why he'd stopped. He replied his teeth had got too loose.

For us a serious problem was the fact that commonly there could be a dense crowd of about 400, which made any action among them potentially hazardous; we tended to run through the crowd, snatch our target, then get out fast to open space. Once there was a sudden outcry and a Black man ran for the mosque exit. We chased, he fell over a box of tomatoes, his knife fell, I dived to grab that, and as he started to run again, one of my Black members, Chili, at a sprint jumped over my shoulder to land feet-first on the man, flattening him into another few boxes of fruit. We thought he'd stabbed or tried to stab someone, but no one complained, so no charge.

Chili, in passing, at any lecture on fingerprinting always used to ask how to bring in specimen fingers from a corpse. The answer is not to cut the fingers off separately but to bring in, if possible, the whole hands, and, if the skin is detaching, to place the fingertips over your own finger and roll the prints.

*

The most hectic New Year's Eve on the beachfront had us involved in three shooting incidents. The first took place in the early evening in the middle of North Beach. My crew and I got there second to find a Black man with a bullet wound in the leg bleeding a fair bit, but keen to complain. We told him an ambo was on its way so he could shut up. The first guys on scene were examining an oldish White woman rolled up next a small braai. Her male friend said she'd shot herself, but there was no sign of a firearm. This finally was found tucked under her chin.

She and her friend, both visibly poor, had come down to braai a short piece of boerewors and a little chop each. The Black guy had shouted at them that they weren't wanted, so she drew her .38 revolver and shot him. She then seemed to have panicked, put the muzzle to her ear and fired. She lasted about 40 minutes, a remarkably long time.

The second was the Indian man shot in the stomach in the *porte cochère* main entrance to the Edward Hotel. As he lay in the driveway, he caused a lot of traffic confusion for an hour or more. As far as I know he survived.

There was a police caravan parked at South Beach to act as a detached Charge Office simply to ease the problems of battling through the huge crowds milling around, and to assist those people. The female on duty there suddenly came on the air to say shots were being fired. We could hear several over the radio. I was in a car driven by a regular Warrant Officer with a Black sergeant with a shotgun in the back. A fast response was needed. We drove down a pedestrian path at 80 kph to the Little Top. The people parted with impressive speed. Once there we jumped out, then zigzagged up the pathway, darting in turn from cover to cover till we reached the caravan with shots still going off. About fifteen of us got there in the first three minutes. No one knew what was going on except that the shooting was on the landward side in or across the gardens. Spontaneously we formed a firing line, jumped up the retaining wall and crawled to the top of the bank guns in hand. Then, nothing. A couple of girls suddenly wandered into the fire zone, didn't understand calls to run and had to be dragged away. Then nothing carried on. Finally we dropped back and uncocked. Thirty or so shots had been fired but I never heard what had happened.

Neither the first nor the third shootings made the papers, the second got a footnote.

*

One of the more unusual business types in the Point area in the early 1980s was the invisible beer shop. These were run by Black women who on the hottest day could supply iced beer on the street side. They filled a 25-litre plastic tub with ice and bottles of beer, which they lowered into a storm-water drain. Each bottle had a length of string around its neck running up to the street through a drainage hole. They operated at night and on Saturday afternoons and Sundays, when the bottle stores were shut, but died out when the shop hours were extended. The most popular area was the Tyzack to Fisher Street part of Point Rd.

*

The Addington area had originally been a series of sand dunes between the Point and the town, which effectively stopped at Cato Creek. This drained the swamp now occupied by the string of sports stadia, the magistrates' courts, the Square, and previously by Stamford Hill aerodrome, into the harbour. They were connected by the railway which ran along what became Farewell Road. In the1860s the young sporting types used to race the train on their horses. The first streets and houses appeared in the 1880s. Some of the residual little lanes had small terrace houses dating from then but occupied by a curious lot.

I once went with Don Vermoter to a reported disturbance there. All seemed quiet, so I knocked on a door. After some odd mutterings and a lengthy removal of chains straight from a Crun scene in a Goon Show, the door opened to reveal two scrawny white women of uncertain age with their skirts tucked up into their underwear, carving knives in their hands and their teeth out. We gathered they were making sandwiches. They told us the disturbance was caused by the rubbishes next door.

*

The first time I walked beat after taking over at Point I found a vagrant apparently sleeping in one of the beachside covered benches. I simply walked up and kicked him neatly on the arch of the foot. He woke at once and, after discussion, moved on. The technique seemed to impress my constable and broke the ice. On another occasion, we found a man lying in a shop entry. He jumped awake with such vigour that his head hit a display window so hard the burglar alarm went off, right next his ear. He landed standing upright. A minute or two later, Radio called us to investigate the alarm. I merely remarked that we had attended and there was no break-in. Stormy nights could be a real nuisance for alarms.

*

I managed to surprise one world-weary cafe owner up Prince Edward St, standing behind the steel mesh grill that protected him behind his counter. Late one night we dragged in a drunk Black guy who had been beaten around the head and was well slathered in blood. We studied his injuries in the light, then I asked for wet paper towels to clean him up. The owner remarked he had never seen that done before by the police.

*

Camden Place was the scene of one unusual disturbance. We found the complainant at the entrance hall of the block. Also there, lying down having hysterics, was a woman, with a couple of other women screaming about some guy up on the third floor. So we went upstairs, urged on by a variety of excited people, to find a guy in a room with the large centre pane of the window largely missing. He was staggering drunk but still full of fight. After a while, we gathered that he'd come home to find his woman being happily screwed on the bed by the complainant. He objected so he pulled the visitor off the woman, beat the shit out of the visitor and threw the woman through the window. She went down three floors but landed on the washing lines, and broke them to land only bruised on the lawn. We arrested him for assault. He absolutely could not believe that he was being arrested. I believe she later withdrew the charges and thought it all rather romantic.

*

A funny murder happened down towards the dock gates one Saturday afternoon. When Godfrey Hamshire and I got there, a Black man was lying on his back on the pavement. He had been shot in the throat by a .38 which left a neat bloodless entry wound in the left side of his throat just above the collarbone. His lungs were still deflating, making a series of bubbles in the blood in his mouth. What made us laugh was the fact that he'd gone off like a champagne bottle, with a thick spray of blood spread at right angles to his body across the ground for about a metre each side of his mouth. We also were astonished when Petty Naidoo, then with six years' service, arrived as back-up, and we found this was the very first murder scene he'd attended.

The shooter was a raw Black from the farm who was a special constable. This was a short-lived emergency unit created to support the SAP, used largely as gate guards. When the police photographer took shots of the scene, he asked the shooter, who claimed the dead guy had threatened him with a knife, to stand in the position where he fired. He absolutely refused to do so. He would not be photographed as he believed his soul would be stolen, and whoever had the photo would have power over him, could put a curse on him. I put a box on the spot and we carried on.

*

Another witchcraft tale involved Godfrey Hamshire's mother. She lived in a fairly isolated house near Port Shepstone with her youngest son, who had Downs Syndrome. There had been a series of housebreakings, not discouraged by a shooting when

Godfrey and his pal Snyders were there and probably killed one of two raiders. Finally, he called in a white healer or witchdoctor for a solution. He put a number of animal and vegetable items, *muti*, in a glass tube and glued this together with a number of seagull feathers over the doors. The robberies stopped. Even the housemaid refused to come, not even to collect outstanding wages.

In a similar case, a tube of *muti* was put over the entrance to a stevedores' hostel. They climbed through the windows until a new doorway was broken out.

The premier division soccer teams reportedly each had a staff witchdoctor who fixed the goals before each match.

Up in the Eastern Transvaal, now Mpumalanga, there used to be a specialist witchcraft unit in the police, as they had about 300 *muti* murders and witch killings a year. In *muti* murders the victims, often children, are killed for body parts, primarily the heart or liver, and sometimes, particularly in Swaziland, after being flayed alive. Witches were looked for to explain sudden deaths or damage from, say, lightning strikes or disease, and then stoned or burned to death.

One of the most bizarre murders in Pinetown was a fake *muti* killing done by a British immigrant who killed his girlfriend and her daughter and cut out various body parts. What he failed to realise was that no Whites were ever killed by Blacks for this purpose.

*

The call came from Radio Control: "Suicide in progress," they told us and gave the address. "The complainant will meet you downstairs." I looked at Petty Naidoo: we raised our eyebrows. We were in uniform dealing with complaints.

When we arrived, a middle-aged Indian man flagged us down: "It's my son-in-law. He's already committed suicide once, is threatening to do it again."

We reached the second-floor flat where a grey-skinned

scrawny man of about twenty-two was sitting in the lounge looking odd, with bulging eyes fixed on mid-air. Petty asked the women – mother, sister, wife – what was going on. He had been threatening to drink a bottle of Dyant, a very lethal poison. This was not visible. "Where is the Dyant? Bring, bring now." Petty was handed the Dyant. He pulled the bottle out of the box, and slapped it down on the coffee table in front of the man. "OK, we've got ten minutes. If you want to commit, drink it but don't waste our time."

The man stared at the bottle. His eyes bulged more, he slumped lower. We stood near at hand but chatted to the family. Apparently he had drunk bleach a couple of months previously, which gave him three weeks in hospital. He seemed to be a mental case but psychiatrists were scarce, expensive, and not effective.

The ten minutes passed. Naidoo took the bottle and emptied it down the kitchen sink with a lot of water. We explained his problem was not one we could solve, and left. Unusually they were Christian Baptists so on the Monday I phoned their parish to ask them to help.

*

We were cruising. I was driving, Godfrey was crew. In the back of the car were two new recruits getting their first outdoors experience as part of their training.

We were drifting along at about 20 kph. Godfrey watching left, me centre and right. Suddenly he said, "Hell, look at that."

I looked left. "Oh shit."

Ahead next the beach on the pavement were two White males. One had a pistol in his right hand and was struggling to pull on a jersey, the pistol flailing all over.

They turned onto the beach heading for the waves. Godfrey and I got out of the car fast and quietly. We drew our pistols, cocked, went over the low wall that held back the sand and chased at a steady jog trot. I went for his gun hand, Godfrey to his left. As I grabbed the gun, Godfrey put his left arm round his throat and his pistol muzzle to his head. "Don't even think about it," he murmured. I plucked the pistol from his hand, ejected the magazine and made safe before the other guy could get a word out. When we got back to the car the new boys were still in the back with no idea what had happened. Mind you, barring our initial exclamations, we had said nothing to each other.

We reckoned we'd do well as muggers.

*

One Saturday night the Square's reservists took over Berea. They were having their annual reservists' braai and the bulk of their regulars would be there too, definitely beyond the calls of duty.

About midnight I took a call from Colchester in England. A man was speaking for a friend whose brother had been killed the other side of Hillcrest. This murder had been in the papers so I knew some details. He was upset that it had taken four days to identify the body. I explained that this had been done from fingerprints in the car, as he'd been necklaced.

"So what," says he.

"I don't think you understand what a necklacing is. You put a tyre or inner tube filled with petrol around the victim's neck, then set fire to it. It is as effective as a cremation except that the ashes get mixed up with the residual rubber and the surface tarmac or gravel."

That ended the complaint.

After making enquiries of Maritzburg Radio Control, I phoned back details of the investigating officer and where and when to call.

*

Most people think that one or two shots are sufficient to kill or at least knock a man down: not so. My father told me of one of their pre-war training movies, taken between the trenches in the First World War. It showed a German officer armed with a sword charging a British officer with a pistol. He was hit in the body by five bullets but managed to reach and cut down the Britisher. I had heard of a man running from a bank robbery taking up to twenty rounds which even went through him to knock chips out of a wall, but still running a hundred metres uphill before dropping.

One of the Reaction Unit guys I knew arrived at a robbery in Westville where one suspect had apparently been wounded but fled the scene. He pursued and was pointed to a set of walled gardens in front of a row of duplexes over a hundred metres away. He climbed on top of the eight-foot-high front wall and ran along till he spotted the man on a lawn. The man tried to shoot him with a handgun so he gave him two rounds in the head. He then worked out that those were the thirty-fifth and thirty-sixth bullets to hit the man.

He also had one of the more scary traffic incidents. A heavy truck went off the freeway bridge at Pigeon Valley and fell about 40m to the river bed. He abseiled down from the bridge to treat the driver. He was stretchered up and my pal was about halfway back up when he felt a violent flutter on his rope and heard a big metallic screech from above. Before he could work out what was going on, a 30-ton truck came off the bridge and fell missing him by three metres.

*

In my early years at the Square we used to patrol the parkland along the Umgeni bank between the Windsor Park golf course and the beach. This was a popular site for picnics or family outings by Indians. Our main object was to discourage robberies, but we also enforced the ban on the drinking of liquor in a public place. We generally never confiscated any booze or made any arrests, but asked them to pack away any unopened stuff and pour out open cans or bottles after taking details and giving formal warnings. Only once did anyone complain, and he shut up when the station commander offered to open a docket against him.

That area at night was not very safe. Cars would pull in, but often the springs carried on or the windows misted up. We could surround a car without anyone noticing. Once we did this, then slapped the roof. When the door fell open, it was obvious that the middle-aged couple had been busy with cunnilingus. I had to admire the man's response: while still on his knees he tried to sell us discounted radios.

*

The nearest I ever came to declaring a child in need of care was at Addington hospital. In terms of the Children's Act, a policeman could remove a child to a place of safety if he found it being abused, starved, used for criminal purposes, drugged or various other things. Maurice Ossendrywer and his crew had gone to a domestic in a flat. A man and his *stukkie* were arguing and fighting across a baby of about twelve months. His parentage was the basis of the argument. They noticed that the only clothes for the baby were two babygros, one on, one off. The only furniture was a mattress. So they took mother and baby to the hospital and asked me to advise. The baby looked OK but we arranged for the emergency paediatric unit to look him over. Three doctors came in and examined him carefully, found no physical damage, and observed him carefully with his mother. All seemed well, but as the mother had a battered face and chest we offered her a bed for the night simply to give her and the baby a break. She refused, just wanted a lift back. I asked if the man would beat her up again if she went back. Yes, she said, but if she stayed away overnight he would beat her up twice as much.

It turned out he was a security guard recently out of jail for assault and rejoiced in the name of Magot.

*

One busy afternoon, we were called to Addington Hospital for a stabbing case. It was my personal record as two of us opened seven dockets in a twelve-hour shift, including thefts – one of three two-metre-tall paintings screwed to the wall in a hotel reception area – a car crash in a parking garage, cheque fraud, forgery and uttering, and last this case. When I reached the ward I found a Coloured woman with a jagged knife slash around her throat from ear to ear with a semi-transparent bandage over it. Not knowing quite what her mood might be, I solemnly asked the ward sister who was at the foot of her bed whether if I made her laugh her head would fall off. She, equally dead-pan, replied no. At this, the woman burst out in a cackle of laughter, the ice was broken and we all got on famously. A docket for attempted rape and attempted murder – she had also been stabbed in the back and stomach – was opened. We took every detail of the people who probably knew her attackers and ultimately two men, total strangers to her, each got seven years.

*

Another dire family I met when called to a domestic, the so-called *pa-slaan-vir-ma*. He was a big former Hell's Angel with all the tattoos, now a forty-going-on-sixty truck driver. She was biggish, flaccid, dark tanned, no make-up, an occasional cashier. We sent him out to sit on the stairs so we could get a clear story from her. Also there were her daughter, fifteen and timid, her boyfriend, a sixteen-year-old rabbit, and two younger children. After some talk it turned out that the violence had gone on for years. She wanted a divorce but was deterred by ignorance of her legal rights and disinformation from her husband; he was also having an incestuous relationship with the daughter. I gave her a crash course in divorce law, details of legal aid and social workers; and a really pointed warning to the husband. On Monday I phoned the boss of the child welfare to report their case.

*

Our views on the press tended to be pretty sceptical. A lot of them, especially the overseas ones, had a very strong bias against us, depicting us as the white fascist agents of the racist regime. We assumed they found this easier as they never came near us. Given the amount of official or open racism prevalent in the UK and the USA until at least the 1960s, we reckoned we were being beaten for their sins. It's not so easy to take a high moral tone with the people in your own street. Another problem was that they viewed us through the prism of their own local or home country situations, which is why they often failed to understand our underlying social and other assumptions. I was once solemnly asked by an American tourist about our minorities. It took some time to explain that the Whites were the minority, but she never understood what I was driving at when I asked what the USA would be like if there had been forty million Indians west of the thirteen colonies. I once spent an evening in Jo'burg in the company of a White American woman reporter for one of their big east coast dailies. She had absolutely no sense of humour and could not tell if the rest of us, including her perhaps obligatory Black boyfriend, were joking or not, which often we were. We simple locals could see at once that he was taking full advantage of her in every possible way, and he knew that we knew, and we knew that he knew that we knew; but she hadn't a clue.

We got no credit for trying to hold together a highly volatile and violent society. In the 1990s the daily average for Durban was seven murders, thirty-five armed robberies and six car hijacks, with about 35 000 reported murders a year in SA. The overseas journos weren't interested in this, while the locals happily took the press officer's daily handout. They seldom bothered us on the street, and I can't recall one ever riding with a complaints van though I have a vague idea one tried to ride with a Dog Unit. On the one occasion I was approached I pointed out I was not an eyewitness, and then proceeded to bore the reporter witless on some irrelevancy. That works like magic.

*

One of the more exotic characters to arrive at the Square was a German artisan. He was dressed in his full late-mediaeval guild costume of dark brown corduroy shorts, waistcoat, and jacket over a linen blouse. His hat was a loose beret, also in cord, and his stout stick over his shoulder carried his kit in a large red and white handkerchief. He was doing his journeyman year travelling the world picking up jobs on the road. I took him up to the German Club in Westville where he made a minor sensation and got plenty of beer and a job.

*

Another dressing up incident involved an Indian found in police uniform in the Point. He claimed to be a reservist from Chatsworth but had no police ID. In any event no out-of-district member ever worked in our area without our knowing about it, and certainly not on his own and in uniform.

I was called in to sort this out. It turned out he had borrowed a friend's uniform and was not a member. I promptly seized all the uniform as exhibits for a charge of theft, alternately, for possession of stolen property, leaving him in the cell in his underpants – much to the satisfaction of the black regulars on duty. He also faced a charge of impersonating a police officer.

*

Only one of my colleagues was tried for murder. That was John Gunnell, a Warrant at Berea. His private business was that of a landlord of a variety of properties. Somehow he got into a dispute with a Portuguese who owned a nightclub and by report dealt in drugs. John refused to be intimidated by this large and wilful type when he called at his office. After a full and frank exchange of views, the Porro tried to strangle him.

John was pushed with his chair head-down into the corner of the room behind his desk, with the other landing on top of him, still strangling him. He pulled his pistol and fired. He could recall firing four shots before he blacked out but he fired two more by instinct, one of which hit the Porro in the head. There was a vengeful mother and six brothers, all large and armed, who kept visiting him. Happily he was able to prove self-defence.

*

I once got from Radio Control the helpful instruction to pick up a Black lunatic in West Street. As West Street was about 3kms long and ran through the main shopping area, I asked for a slightly more precise spot and a description. They suggested near the Pine Street crossing but could help no further. Strangely we found him, and told him his mother was worried and he must come, which he did. At King Edward VIII Hospital, we walked him to the psychiatric ward. The nurses were stocky, strong, but short Zulu women. They asked us to stay till he'd been sedated. The inch-thick steel bars over the windows up to 12 feet above the floor had been battered out of shape, apparently by patients wielding beds. Our man whispered that he wanted to show me where the nurses boiled badly behaved patients after sliding them down a chute. He took me to a little room, and there was the chute. On the door though was a sign reading "laundry".

Back in the ward they gave him a quarter-pint injection of a schedule nine sedative in his bottom. He started to squeal so I told him: "*Thula*, take it like a man." He actually shut up so I remarked to my crew: "He must be insane."

*

As a general rule, we operated only inside the borders of the area of our station, and very seldom outside our district unless invited for a specific job. This did not stop us running across the boundaries if in hot pursuit, though again, this was uncommon. The only time I went into Wentworth, a Coloured suburb next the Bluff in the Durban South area, was to take home an eleven-year-old boy we had picked up on the beachfront. It turned out he was the despair of his family and had climbed down the drainpipe from his locked bedroom in their third-floor flat. Wentworth had been built on an English 1950s-style model: blocks of flats in sweeping parkland with pedestrian walkways. The grass, then knee- to waist-length, concealed the broken or missing steps on the paths; while attack dogs running on long chains could reach many pathways, and most lights were smashed or shot out. To top it off, gangs ran the place, with the police station, as I recall, on the border of the territories of the K9s and the Green Vultures. We parked our van facing outwards with Raggie at the wheel and with the engine running. No one was surprised when I remarked that, if I was forced to move there, I'd drive to the airport, dump my car, and take the first plane out.

*

Domestic violence was a continual problem that did not lend itself to police intervention, either in individual cases or as a broad category. In what could be loosely described as endurable assaults, our problem simply was that even if the assault was reported, the complaint in the vast majority of cases would be withdrawn. The motive for this ranged from the weepy making up, not uncommon in drunken assaults, to sheer terror, to the wife blaming herself for the beating. One memorable instance was where an NGK minister in Westville beat up his wife with a ploughshare out in their garden. Their neighbours called it in, but she refused to complain.

Some wives though did try to stop it. There was a procedure known as a restraining order which a wife could go to the magistrate's court to get. This did have some value as proof of violence in later divorce or custody cases, but generally got little respect from the men. I came across instances where the husband tore the order into confetti, sprinkled it over her head, then flattened her. The men as a rule were bullies and real shits, but also cowards. My advice on occasion was that the woman should get an upholsterer's needle and sew the man, while asleep, to his mattress and the bed; then either flog him with a sjambok, or if she really hated him, gag him and go on holiday for a couple of weeks.

*

Men did get beatings from wives, but, out of shame presumably, they never came near us. Once when taking divorce instructions I remarked to the wife that she had not mentioned any drunkenness or violence against her. Oh there was – once. It turned out he had once knocked her down, but she grabbed a Murano glass ashtray that weighed about three pounds, threw it and broke his ankle.

*

The women I felt desperately sorry for were those with small children, whose options for escape were often limited by lack of money, fear for the youngsters, or lack of family back-up. There was no refuge in Durban for them, until a pastor managed to get the loan of part of an old primary school in Point. He begged or borrowed beds and other basic furniture, as well as food discarded by supermarkets and others. He managed to accommodate about a dozen women and their children. He had little or no official backing, running into bureaucrats at every turn. We reservists and regulars helped in various ways. We routinely looked in to make sure they were safe. I advised the women where to go, who to see, and how they could get help. Some of the members helped get food and clothes. Underlying everything was the status of the school buildings. He had got lucky while the question wandered from one provincial department to another, while central government also popped up to create an agenda gridlock. But they typically were not efficient in their inefficiency, and sometime after I left Point the school turned into an archive or storage place, and his brave effort dissolved.

*

In the mid-1980s we had a number of terrorist bomb blasts in Durban. We were therefore always alert to the possibility and kept our eyes open. If we found something suspicious, we would clear the area and call in the bomb squad, preferably from a spot around a solid wall. There was a risk that the bomb might be set off by our radio transmissions as remote-controlled-car components had been used as triggers. The night Magoo's Bar was attacked, I felt the blast through my feet some 4kms away. That killed two and injured several.

The nearest I came to a blast was one morning at the office, when one of our secretaries came in late and looking rather shocked. A bomb had been set off on the Esplanade opposite John Ross House, a fourteen-storey block in which she had a flat. The entire glass façade was sucked off the building and fell like a waterfall into the playground of a crèche, which a quarter of an hour later would have been full of toddlers. The funny bit was that the only two killed were two ANC supporters who had been waiting for a lift.

*

There were also social and racial inhibitions that operated. Indian and Coloured members were often diffident about arresting Whites, and Blacks all the more so, simply from social habit or because they'd be told they were arresting nobody and to fuck off; or they'd be threatened with the divisional or national commissioner of police, an MP or some such. To the occasional joy of my members, I had no qualms about arresting anyone in town, nor did some of the other Whites and a couple of Indians. I had at least seriously threatened to arrest advocates, businessmen, prosecutors, regular policemen, even a diplomat. When threatened with a celebrity, I generally asked if they were confident that their connection would gamble his pension for them, and offered to copy the docket to him.

On the other hand, each of us had our own special knowledge from our jobs, social position and languages. I needed Zulu speakers for street work. Indian members often had social or business connections of interest or use. Female members were often better suited for child protection or rape cases. This was simply a reflection of the then current social and economic patterns in Durban.

*

I took the view that every member should be able to go home after every shift with something to brag about, something worthwhile he had done. This helped to keep his family onside, because if they thought he was risking himself to no real purpose, he would soon agree with them and fade away. Starting at the Square I made a point of asking for suggestions from my members for problem areas or events we could police. This both gave them a chance to shine in their own communities, and made them think about what we should be doing. It was also perhaps refreshing to be treated as valuable members.

After spending hours as a constable standing around while the guys in charge tried to work out what to do with us, I made sure any static time took place next to a cafe or somewhere they could get a drink. At Point we dubbed the Excel Cafe, the all-night place on the beachfront, our detached tactical HQ. It sounded much better on the radio and the mike operators seldom caught on. None of us was paid so a sense of adventure was vital. At Point it was sometimes debated at about 3 am at the Excel why we did it. The consensus was that we were all adrenaline junkies. That was a good time for a pitstop, in the lull between pub and nightclub chuck-outs. A favourite snack was a large ashet of chips with a couple of ladles of thick curry gravy over them, shared between six or more, each with fork in hand. At the signal everyone fell to in a stabbing frenzy that lasted perhaps sixty seconds. This turned into an informal welcoming – or initiation – party for recruits newly on the street.

Mind you, the Excel was not a crime-free zone. Our record for a coffee break was two arrests and finding a runaway girl. One night, one of the customers ordered a toasted cheese sandwich. He was dissatisfied, so he went home, fetched his pistol, and shot the waiter dead.

At the Square, we sometimes shared an executive bunnychow, that is, a whole loaf shared by a patrol of five or six. A bunnychow is a chunk of bread hollowed out, filled with stew or curry, and the bread put back on top to mop up the gravy. With care, you can eat it without a spot of gravy on your fingers. Made well, as at the Royal Hotel, it can be delicious; made badly you can get a grease bunny.

The worst food I ever tasted was a packet of curried chips from an iffy cafe up Grey Street way. The very *slap* chips were put in a bag, then curry powder thrown on. The chips were so *slap* that I could stir them with my finger into a sludge. Not even a grease bunny could beat this.

Eating and drinking on duty could be a problem. Quite a few cafes were happy to encourage police visits by giving free tea, coffee or cool drinks from the vat. Cans of drink or food we would pay for. At Albert Park we often had tea and cream scones – not fierce food. I once caused some alarm by wandering into the Mayfair (a central hotel) with two others with rifle, shotgun, sidearms, gas and all, to ask for tea and little pink cakes, which they couldn't supply: Bother! I drew the line at free meals as this could be a form of bribery. One sleazy hotel near Albert Park tried this, but then he also rented by the hour. The one exception was the debutante balls at the city hall where plates of breyani were cheerfully given. These, though, were organised like school dances with no long-term commercial issues.

*

One type of theft that we did not have much of was the theft of building materials. Builders I knew found this a real nuisance. One, working in a Black township, in despair after having his arm broken by thieves, went to see the neighbouring warlord to ask for his help as they were running into his area. He simply replied, "Why don't you kill them?"

The most spectacular theft was in Port Elizabeth when, over a weekend, a school building catering for some 400 pupils was completely stolen, leaving only the foundation footings.

The practical effect of this was that when a house in a township was nearing completion and handover, on the last day the builder would fit the windows; the kitchen and bathroom plumbing and fittings; hang the doors; install the electrical wiring, ceiling boards and floor tiles; slap on the paint; and hand over the keys. After that it was the owner's problem. Township dwellers never, if at all possible, left their houses empty for, say, a holiday.

*

Another crime more talked of than encountered was rape to order. In the normal course of events we seldom had to deal with rape of any type. It was half jocularly rumoured though that the going rate for a corrective gang rape was R100 plus a crate of cane spirit, or if she was really ugly, two crates.

*

While as a rule reservists were keen to make arrests, we did not pursue this relentlessly but used our common sense and discretion to solve the problem with the minimum disruption or long-term damage, provided the people did not have a bad attitude.

*

It was an assault next to the Excel; a headbutt, spectacles broken, loose teeth, a splash of blood. Nothing unusual, except that the headbutter had an honours degree in psychology and was doing his practical year before being licensed to practice. If he was convicted of assault with intent to do grievous bodily harm – GBH – his career would probably be over before it started. He was only too aware of this. He was staring into the abyss. The other guy was a plain, ordinary bloke, still a bit stunned by it all, but not particularly determined to make a complaint. So we all went back to the station to discuss the situation.

I settled matters on the basis that no formal complaint would be laid; that the psychologist would pay for new spectacles, and damages of R3 000,00 within thirty days; and that he consented to a civil court judgement on non-payment. Each got a signed copy of the written agreement. I promised not to mention this to the psychologist's cousins, who to his horror had been classmates of mine at school.

*

At the Square one night, a crew of our members brought in a car and five Indian medical students in custody. They had been parked in an oddly shady spot. When our car approached, the students threw something from their car and drove off. They were stopped. The packet was found, opened and found to be a hand of dagga. A hand was a quantity of loose dagga about the size of a small loaf. This was sufficient to convict all five of possession and for the car to be seized and sold. This would really have annoyed one lucky father, but also would have given each a drugs conviction, which would have killed off their careers and stopped them emigrating to anywhere worthwhile. The regular Warrant Officer in charge and I discussed this while the troops were writing the docket and interviewing the students. He took the view that the potential damage vastly outweighed the offence, and despite our enthusiasm I agreed. We therefore carried on very slowly writing up, taking names and addresses of parents, professors, and all, fingerprinting and processing them. This took the better part of two hours, during which they had plenty of time to contemplate the loss of up to five years of study, and a very bleak future, and that all for some stupid dare. Finally I told them we had decided not to charge them: they could go and take their car. I doubt they tried that again.

*

Another night there was a Boy George lookalike competition. Our van crews at the Square got involved when they spilled out into the street with their beers. Soon we had a row of sixteen-year-olds against the Charge Office wall. We merely warned them, but phoned their parents to collect them. One father, not thrilled to come thirty km at 2 am, walked in, glanced at the row, then asked where his son was. We pointed him out. He did a double-take, then curled his index finger: "Come."

Junior had to trot to keep up as father headed back to the car. "Pa, pa, I can explain … "

Whack. "*Eina, pa!*" Squeal of tyres.

*

One useful ability for a policeman is to be able to persuade people to co-operate with a minimum of drama, whether through fisticuffs or paperwork. To judge by TV, this is equally useful for politicians although they cannot normally themselves lock up anyone unconvinced.

*

A Saturday night at the Square: a couple of law students or articled clerks were pulled in for drinking in public. Their pals turned up to try to talk them free. Legal arguments were forcefully advanced; habeas corpus was invoked. The regular Warrant in charge, a nice guy but not up to subtle legal debate in English against a dozen, was floundering so I wandered over also in uniform. One of the main speakers was wearing a Wits Law T-shirt.

"Are you doing articles?"

"Yes."

"Oh, which firm are you with?"

He named them.

"Oh yes, they're a good firm. Who's your principal?"

He named him.

"Yes, he's a nice guy, a good attorney. I see him quite often. What's your name so I can mention you to him?"

A pause.

Then from the back of the group: "Pay the man his money and let's go."

And after a collection they went.

*

Knock on window of car with out-of-province plates in Fisher St: "Good evening sirs. I see you're on holiday here. I hope you'll have a good time. Just a word of warning though: with the girls here you have only a 6 to 8% chance of getting Aids. For a 50 to 60% chance you should go to the truck park which is ..."

The car leaves fast.

I turn with a grin to receive the f*** offs of the street whores.

*

We came across a stag party of seven having a raucous time. We strolled over. "Could you keep the volume down a bit?"

"But we're not making a noise are we?" says one.

"No way!" chorused his mates.

"Yes you are."

"So what are you going to do about it? You do know who we are?"

"Yes." I looked them over. "Most of you are prosecutors."

"That's right, and you know where your docket will end up."

"Yes: the original to the Control Magistrate, a duplicate to the Deputy Assistant Attorney-General, both by hand and receipted, and a further copy retained."

A slight pause.

"OK chief, we'll be good."

And they were.

*

There was an odd follow-up to this. A few months later I was on my way to the Supreme Court, when I met one who was now a junior advocate. We chatted and he asked if I was giving evidence that morning.

"No," I said, "I've got a divorce case."

"Oh," said he in surprise, "are you an attorney?"

When I agreed he looked rather pensive, recalling no doubt that in effect only attorneys could hire him.

*

One car chase we did win. I cut off the second car in the chase. The driver jumped out and started swearing us. My driver Bertolotti, filled with youthful zeal, wanted to flatten him but I waved him back. Instead I stood next our car, checked my watch, and timed his swearing. At last he paused to draw breath. "One minute forty-three seconds: not bad but rather repetitive. Can I suggest a few phrases?" After a few deep breaths he started talking rationally.

*

Police humour tended to be of a somewhat unsociable type. In mixed company we tended to find ourselves at one end of the room, with the civilians at the other; but cracking jokes and drinking coffee while standing next to a cooling corpse tends to inform your style.

*

On the beachfront one night we were driving off feral black kids – runaways living on their wits, aged from about seven upwards. They were a pest, begging, stealing and taking money for parking. If you didn't tip, you risked finding your car scratched. I asked Cst Busane, a good cop and a brave one, to take one down the pier and tell him to walk to Australia. He nodded soberly, took the kid by the arm and headed for the pier. As they climbed onto the pier and walked steadily down it I remarked to my back-up man Bertolotti, "I hope Busane has a sense of humour ..."

*

"Hey South Africa's now a democracy."

"Correct, you can now choose. Do you want to get in the van with or without broken legs?"

*

"*Sawubona amadoda*, what are you doing here?" asks Hamshire in a friendly fashion late one night.

"We are waiting for the combi."

"Do you have your oxygen permits?"

"E... oxygets what?

"Yes yes, it's a new thing to stop people stealing oxygen. Come, produce!"

Various puzzled mutters in Zulu – what is this stupid *mlungu* talking about? – yes he is an idiot but he is a cop – I do not need this shit in my life – let's humour the bloody fool and lose him. Finally they dig in their wallets and find some papers, any papers.

"No, these are not correct. Last month's permit was white, this month's is green. Go fetch and tomorrow you must show me."

That's one way to clear the street.

*

Cst Koos van der Merwe gets a phone call. He is told that Koekemoer has been killed in a car crash. Can he please go and give his wife the sad news. So he knocks on her door. She opens it.

"*Is u die weduwee Koekemoer?*" [Are you the widow Koekemoer?]

"*Nee.*" [No.]

"*Moenie vir my f***** lieg nie dame!*" [Don't f****** lie to me, lady!]

This naturally causes a lot of upset. Vd Merwe's boss calls him in, *kak hom kollosaal uit* [tells him off firmly] and tells him to use some tact, some discretion, be less direct.

Time passes, Koos reflects. Then comes the news that Van Tonder's wife has died. Van Tonder is a member of his relief, so when the squad parades on at the end of their shift, vd Merwe orders: "*Alle getroude mans een pas vorentoe, loop – Van Tonder wat die f** maak jy?!*" [All married men one step forward, march – Van Tonder, what the f*** are you doing?!]

*

Swearing someone's mother was a pretty routine way of being really offensive. The best one I heard, and appropriate to a city with a thriving harbour full of sailors, was "Your mother swims off to ships."

*

In court a rape complainant was being cross-examined. This is a true story.

"I notice that you say you were raped on Monday but you only laid the complaint on the Thursday. Is that correct?"

"Yes."

"Why did you only do it then?"

"The cheque bounced."

*

Alvin Geschwindt started one standing joke. As he and I, and others, set out on a uniform foot patrol, he asked if he could walk next to me. I said sure, but thinking perhaps he had in mind a Laurel and Hardy tribute act, asked why? Oh says he, if we meet the bad guys they'll be sure to aim for you, so I'll be safe. Yes, says I, they'll aim for me but they'll be such rotten shots that they'll hit you. And so we strolled off, both laughing.

Chapter 5

WORKING WITH OTHER BODIES

Child Protection

When I was a sergeant at the Square I and a few others got involved with the start of the first Child Abuse Unit in the country, later more positively called the Child Protection Unit. A teacher at Glenwood High School called Grant Robinson had become concerned about the lack of police focus on child molestation cases, so he joined the force to set up a pilot unit. At that time it was generally known that such cases did sometimes happen, but they attracted little attention and were largely left to social workers to sort out as most witnesses were children. Grant, now a sergeant, was given two constables. To set the unit up they had to collect as much data as possible, simply because little better than rumour was known. He got a rather chilly response from the regulars so he asked us and other Reserve Units to help. Our work consisted among other things of observation of a reported pick-up point for homosexuals in a parking lot outside the nurses' home at Addington. One night there, I watched in fascination from a bus shelter as three cars arrived at 20:45 almost in formation, to park in a row with two empty bays between each of them, with their backs to the nurses. I took note of the car registrations and descriptions of the drivers who were a sorry-looking trio.

After a few months he made a breakthrough, when a boy of

14 decided he would make more money by denouncing some paedophiles. This led to searches which found photo albums. This proved to be common behaviour among paedophiles, keeping trophies. The boy made a small fortune by identifying people in the photos. That led to more searches. Soon over 330 arrests had been made across SA. They simply ran out of policemen to handle any more.

A common problem was that the kids did it for money. As long as the men paid enough they were pretty safe. The unit, for example, knew of one teacher in a reputable school who paid over the odds, despite his headmaster's horrified denials of any such possibility, so he was never prosecuted. I believe he emigrated.

The paedophiles were not popular. One seen by a colleague when held in a Reef jail had over a hundred visible burns on him. The prisoners and the warders had decided that anyone passing him could stub out a cigarette on him. If he argued, they grabbed him and used up the rest of the pack.

Within a few years, the units had been set up in every division. The female major in charge of the Durban unit once memorably started a lecture with: "Every day, all day, in my office and out, all I think about is sex." Service in the units was prone to bend the character of the members after a year or two. One guy I knew resigned after his fiancée told him he was going very strange, and it was the job or her.

Dog Unit

One unit we worked with, but only on occasion, was the Dog Unit. Their main local kennels and training school were behind the Square. About thirty to fifty dogs were there at any one time; most were attack and tracker dogs, some doubled as explosives dogs, plus there were a few sniffer dogs for drugs. These had various specialities: one in Hermanus was used to find *perlemoen* or abalone, which was dried and smuggled out to China. The dogs were very good. They could sniff out one or two bullets in a car from the outside. They could also clear crowds very effectively. A common tactic was to surround a building with a housebreaker inside, put a dog inside and wait. They were the glamour unit, always at the point of breakdown, and going up against the seriously bad, armed or dangerous. The handlers had a very close relationship with their dogs as they teamed up for life, with the retired dogs commonly staying with them as house pets. The only way to deal with dogs like these is to stand very still. Then they'll sit and watch you; if you move fastish, then they'll attack. The bruising left by a bite is much worse than the bite itself, as the pressure at the tip of a fang is about 50 tons per sq in: you won't move happily for two weeks. And, yes, they do bite policemen.

The most dogs I ever had to negotiate were the six in the lane next my office when an occupation of the British Consulate was broken. Denise McCormack had come around to see me, so our progress up the road together was like the children's game of Statues.

Perhaps the most argumentative guy I ever saw brought in by a Dog Unit to the Square, had been spotted driving at speed on the wrong side of the northern freeway while trying to boot his girlfriend out the passenger door. He was chased down by the dog. As he tried to fight it he was deckle-edged from his right shoulder to his knee. Even when he was dragged into the grill room behind the Charge Office he tried to kick the arresting officer in the balls. Only when the dog handler threatened to stamp on his bites did he shut up and calm down.

Security Police
A unit we didn't work with, to the extent that I could recognise possibly one only at a time, was the Security Police. Their base was on the top three floors of the Square. They had their own secure lift from the basement. Though you could walk up the

stairs from the floor below, the entrance was screened by steel walls while the doorway, also steel, was an airlock type watched by the guard through cameras. Ordinary police simply did not go in.

Ambulance Crews
Our relationship with the paramedics in the ambulance crews was necessarily close and complementary as we often found ourselves at the same scenes whether murders, assaults or motor collisions. We were always conscious of the need to protect them. Added to this, I had a couple of members who were themselves paramedics, notably Roland and Matthew Dunstan, who were old boys of Michaelhouse, a prestigious private boarding-school in inland Natal. Rather unusually at one point there were three OMs and a Kearsney (a similar school) old boy at Point which did add a little touch of *klaas*.

One of my early and illuminating encounters with the ambo service happened one night near the Berea Road taxi ranks when Chili and I found a Black male lying drunk in the gutter and bleeding from both ears. This is an indication of a serious head wound, probably with subcranial bleeding, that at a minimum should need a day or two in hospital for observation and diagnosis. He revived and we tried to persuade him to go to hospital. He refused so, in a fit of innocent zeal, I decided to take him to the nearby ambulance station. Chili and I wrestled him there by brute force. It was the only time I had a button torn off my polyester twill uniform safari tunic. The ambo crew told us they could not treat him unless he agreed, but suggested that next time we knock him out first.

Another early one: I found a Black male lying in heavy rain, stabbed, in a gutter with his blood trickling about twenty metres down the road. What was really odd was that his ID gave his name as (the stereotypically Afrikaans) Van der Merwe.

Odd again was an unconscious Black man I saw being

offloaded one sunny Saturday afternoon from a bus down from Currie's Fountain. We searched his pockets but the only thing on him was a second-hand bus ticket, so he must have been robbed. An ambo came and loaded him up for King Edward VIII hospital. A bit later, we went there to follow up on the case. There was no record of him there at all. The reception clerks there were generally anti-police but there was a record of that ambo delivering another man there. What had happened to our man? After a while I tracked one of the crew back to his home to find that, when they opened the back to put in another casualty at Albert Park, he sat up, jumped out and sprinted off madly in the general direction of Congella.

As a rule the ambos got to a call very quickly. The only real exception was a stabbing victim, as usual a Black man, who I found unconscious near the market. When no one had arrived yet nearly an hour after the first call, I threatened to charge their radio operator with culpable homicide if he died. Coincidentally an ambo arrived within five minutes.

Hospitals

We often had occasion to go to the casualty departments of the local hospitals, usually Addington, or King Edward VIII, which was the Black hospital in Umbilo, either taking victims of assaults or following up on victims taken in by ambos, either to interview them or at the least to get their hospital patient numbers if they were unconscious or unidentified. Generally we got on well with the nurses who, like us, had an unillusioned view of humanity. Sometimes we had to protect them against knifemen, or lunatics, or violent drunks.

In one memorable incident, a teenage Indian gangster was knifed in a daytime nightclub and brought in to Addington by his gang. His rivals arrived soon after to finish him off and the two gangs chased each other all over the complex, some ending up on the fifth floor of the nurses' home.

One night I spent three hours of frustration at Addington trying to get a urine sample for diagnosis from a prisoner who was complaining of pain around the kidneys. After he had drunk but refused to co-operate for an hour or so, the male nurse hooked him up to a pressured one-litre bag of saline. Even then he refused until threatened with a catheter. This I had to do as we were responsible for his well-being after his arrest. As Point only held people briefly this wasn't too often a problem, but where there were cells, such as at the Square or Berea, the cells were visited hourly to check. One night shift at the latter when I asked in the first cell, which held twenty, they said a man in the other cell was sick. It turned out that he was passing blood in his urine, so I sent him under guard to King Edward VIII for treatment. At the Square one Saturday an elderly woman came in to ask if her grandson had been arrested, and had he got his medicine. He had been brought in on a minor charge by the previous shift but was still in the grill sitting sleeping. We couldn't fully wake him and could find no pills for him or on him. As a result I released him into his grandmother's care so she could get him to his doctor.

Some of the more spectacular injuries came from pangas and axes, or glass and bottles, plus of course the carnage from motor crashes. The first group quite often needed three levels of stitching. One cheery anecdote concerned a man waiting in casualty sitting with his chin on his hand. He irritated the orderly by mumbling replies till the orderly slapped his hand away – only for his whole jaw to fall onto his chest as he had taken a panga through the mouth.

One of my more memorable cases was in Pretoria when a Black guy was brought to us articled clerks as he had to go to the Supreme Court, and this worried him. I asked for his story. His sister had loaned money to a certain man, who then repeatedly refused to pay. She asked his help, so he went to the man's parents' house. The man was there chopping firewood. When he again refused to pay, our man said he'd have to tell his parents. So what happened? He hit me. With what? The axe. Where? On the head. At this I looked at him carefully but he looked all right. He then bent his head forward to show a slot across the centre of his skull I could have laid a finger in. I could see him change his mind. He said he did get headaches and at times black spots in front of his eyes. He'd been a hospital outpatient for a couple of weeks. I told him it was a murder trial and he was the victim.

A broken bottle twisted into the face leaves a circular scar perhaps a centimetre wide, but a shard can kill if delivered in the throat, armpit or groin. The circular cut could easily cut out a plug of skin about half a centimetre thick which we would bring in to be stitched back, in a glass of water if possible. Traffic casualties included people impaled on lengths of chrome trim.

Places of Safety
These were designed to be just that, for children in danger from their parents or others, or lost or abandoned. To a large extent they served as entry points into the main child welfare system. Initially they were set up for separate races, but in the early 1990s these distinctions fell away. While this may have had some merit in principle, the effect on the White places was to destroy their function as refuges, as at the same time the police were instructed not to hold juvenile criminals in the cells but to use the places of safety. As a result, victimised children found themselves in dormitories with robbers, drug dealers and the occasional murderer, while the surrounding wall was knee-high. And to cap it all, there were only 354 places in the whole of the Durban metropolitan area. As there were probably thousands of feral black children in the city the system was totally overwhelmed – to our immense frustration.

Radio Station

Radio communications in the Durban area were run from the Square. Generally two frequencies were used: one for Central and South, the other for North and West. The handsets could carry ten channels; the other eight were used for particular operations such as street sweeping or crime prevention operations that were not reliant on the mike operators, as the complaints vans were. Those basically were sent out to incidents reported to Radio, and reported back on completion. One limitation of the system was that only one handset could transmit at a time on each channel which on a busy night could make it hard to get through. Every single radio was assigned a call sign while on the air. For example Point's complaints vans would be DP1 or 2; the station commander's personal call sign was DP10; while mine as branch commander was DP40, with my members taking 41, 42, etc. Active call signs and channels were noted both at Radio and in members' individual pocket books.

The mike operators were backed up by half a dozen telephone operators who took the incoming calls, while a Warrant supervised the whole. I did a number of shifts on the phones until my rank became too high. While the range of complaints was huge, the worst I had was a call from an Indian reporting an attempted break-in at his house. He had a very thick *charro* accent which was made worse by the fact that his street had a rare and complicated Scots name. I had to make him spell it out, as I could hardly hear him for the robbers or assassins breaking down his front door with sledgehammers and axes.

The Morgue

We all knew where this was, up in Gale Street in Umbilo, but no one really went there by choice. We preferred to restrict our contact to the mortuary van crews. I was threatened once or twice in my early days with a visit to an autopsy, but somehow that did not happen. Apparently one pathologist's party piece, after opening the torso, was to whip out all the connected internal organs from the throat to the colon with a single dramatic flourish.

Later I invited a pathologist to give lectures on topics like bullet types and wounds, but he just used photographs and the like for demonstrations. I did once do a tour of the place, including the fridge, which did not have discreet steel drawers but a bank of wooden racks. Most of the bodies were of Black kids dead of gastro-enteritis. The worst aspect though was the smell that permeated the whole place, even the offices. The one sergeant there who said he liked the graft and the two extra salary notches he got, did admit he always had to shower, wash his hair and change to get rid of the reek. It is very distinctive, so I was seriously put off a couple of weeks later to get a whiff of it from a supermarket fish counter.

The Police Garage
All police vehicles were supposed to be repaired and maintained by the police garage which was over towards the Bluff. It was however so inefficient and slow that most station commanders did not maintain their vans and cars there, but made some unofficial local arrangement to keep them going as long as possible. The simplest was just to ignore all routine maintenance. Vehicles often needed nursing to keep operating. The garage seemed to run on the basis of a zero-parts store, which meant they ordered up individual parts when needed from Pretoria, and they were not commercially minded. In addition, the garage was normally short of decent mechanics, and would virtually close for several days when inspections loomed so they could clean the workshop and paint pretty lines on the floor. A van could be held up for weeks or months, allegedly even for wiper blades. As vehicles were at best always in short supply, stations could be seriously embarrassed for

transport. It was common for the whole of Central Durban (District 46) to have only six vehicles with twelve members from five stations to deal with all complaints for a population of between a quarter and a half million people, depending on the time of day. Some nights that fell to four vans when there should have been twelve or more.

SANAB

The SA Narcotics Bureau was the drug squad. It operated as a separate unit tasked with the fight against drugs. The biggest by far was locally grown dagga (marijuana), followed by mandrax, which was largely smuggled in from India through Zambia (probably by ANC members) and smoked with dagga, and then various pharmaceutical prescription drugs, ranging from cough medicine upwards, to LSD and heroin. Dagga was grown as a cash crop, especially in the Midlands and Zululand, so seizures of truckloads of the leaf and sacks of the seed were not uncommon. In my day, cocaine was coming in but was largely a rich man's drug.

SANAB were a rather secretive group and not particularly popular among the uniformed cops. They tended to take the credit in the press for any big drug seizures, no matter who made the actual find. We also, on occasion, found our drug cases spiked by them, as the people we arrested were their informants. At Point we suspected that our members' details were leaked after a couple of unusually good arrests were followed by strange calls on their private phones, and possible tailing of their private cars. At one stage, SANAB let it be known that they were not interested in small retail seizures; so I told that to the Point members, and remarked to general satisfaction that of course there were none of our seizures that were *not* retail. A year or so after I had left the force the local head of SANAB was arrested for corruption, which rather answered our doubts.

Foreign Forces

An officer on holiday from a murder squad in one of the British forces was having a few beers in the officers' mess at the Square with his opposite numbers from the Murder and Robbery Unit. They asked him to explain his methods, which they had glimpsed from news items. This he did. He ran through the temporary command centres, the house to house enquiries, the searching, but above all the sheer numbers of men and resources given to the investigation.

Everyone was impressed; then one asked, "What do you do with the second one that day?"

The visitor was rather nonplussed and started to explain that it had never happened.

At this, the questions went around the group – and the third? And the fourth? And the fifth? And the sixth? And the seventh?

I met a policeman from Liechtenstein, a country I had once walked halfway across by accident when looking for the railway station. It is half an Alpine valley, with the border with Switzerland running along the river. The whole place is about 16 by 8 km. I asked how they managed any car pursuits. "Oh," he said, "that's easy: we phone the Swiss and they block the two bridges."

The Religious

Relations between the various religions and churches and the police could be many and various. They depended both on the church and the individual cleric, but primarily on their political views. All of them would have conceded that a police force was necessary, but some made it pretty clear they would not have chosen us – not that they were ever so clear about who they did want. We, in turn, were rather sceptical about their comments, which not uncommonly arose from an unconquerable amalgam of idealism and ignorance, rather than conscious enmity. Others were pro-police, sometimes excessively so. There were also police chaplains and the occasional imam. They had the unhappy job of informing families of police casualties.

One night I found a black man hiding in a church poorbox. He was arrested for trespass. Admittedly, the box was big enough to take blankets. This was during a regular check of a local church and its cemetery which were much affected by housebreakings, malicious injury to property and thefts, largely by junkies or vagrants. This minister was grateful.

The neighbouring priest though wrote equally often to complain of the police harassing the poor and destroying their goods. The problem was that a lot of homeless blacks used to sleep in a park, making fires and fouling the place. On Friday afternoons the regulars would go there, gather up the debris (pallet bases and plastic sheeting were popular), and ask if anyone owned them. As no one wanted to be arrested for littering there was never more than a few mutters of *"Angaz' "* (that is the Zulu for "Dunno"). So everything, being abandoned goods, was burned; and the complaint arrived on Tuesday.

The Catholic Cathedral was built in about 1880 on what was then the edge of town. No longer: now it was next the Grey Street area, surrounded by nondescript buildings. An informal market for herbal, or if you prefer, witchdoctor remedies operated along the pavement opposite it during the day, while at night the unkempt graveyard was used by drunks and drugtakers.

I once attended a christening there by invitation during a duty shift, which caused a certain disquiet among those who didn't know me as I walked in uniform the full length of the nave. Mind you, I had just driven out of the main entrance a couple of screaming Black female drunks who were shattering the ambience.

Another night, we came on a man lying unconscious next the graveyard, drunk or drugged. I had just checked his condition by a brisk kick to the arch of his foot, when I noticed a priest behind me watching with interest. I waited for the complaint, the denunciation of the brutal police. None came. He was of the view that junkies like this could with advantage be dropped off five miles out to sea, and left to walk home.

This was definitely not the view of Archbishop Hurley who was a committed "liberal". After one pungent speech in which he held forth on oppression, poverty and justice, he started to find his front lawn filled with deserving vagrants every morning looking for the food and clothing promised. The night shift were dropping them there, saying: "Ask this good man. He will give you for to eat." Apparently this led to an unofficial complaint to the police, a complaint that did not reach the newspapers.

I once had occasion to visit the archdiocesan offices. Curiously, the nuns working in the offices were white; the nuns cleaning the offices were black.

The Public
The attitude of the public towards the police was rather ambivalent, and varied widely from group to group. We were seldom popular with the people we arrested, but generally the ones who benefited from those arrests were on our side. However, among some English speakers – notably the swimming pool liberals – there was a sniffiness arising from anti-Afrikaner and racial snobberies, and political postures exacerbated by their almost total irrelevancy to the really powerful political groupings. Afrikaners were nearly all on our side. Among Indians we were generally fairly popular, though they did not want to become too intimate. For most Blacks, we were to a greater or lesser extent a necessary evil, with the Inkhatha more friendly than the ANC who positively regarded us as the enemy. Attitudes on an individual basis, though, were largely influenced by personal experience.

Members of the Reserve had a dual role. We were of course

members of the public for most of our working day, so we tended to see both sides of the story. As a result, we mostly felt no unconditional loyalty to the police right or wrong, but could – and did – take with the public perhaps a more diplomatic approach. I often found myself in the position of explaining how and why the police acted and had to act in the ways they did, and the very real limits to our manpower and equipment. Similarly I could tell the regulars how the public thought of them. One practical problem they had was that they met too many rubbishes and not enough decent people. The result was that often they expected hostility and thus found it.

Public reactions could switch very fast. One night next the town hall we were in plain-clothes trying to arrest or drive off groups of feral black kids who were being a bloody nuisance to people in the street by begging in an intimidating way and stealing if the chance arose. I enticed one in close by pretending to get money for him from my purse. My female backup grabbed and cuffed him. A white woman demanded to know what we were doing to the child. I explained. "Oh", says she, "give him a good smack for me too." That night, one of those we collared ran but was recaptured, so he was handcuffed to a tree. He turned out to be wanted in Tongaat for culpable homicide though he was only fifteen.

Similarly one night I was on foot in plain-clothes with Bernard Lancaster. We had spent some hours detaining black runaway children around the beachfront, some thirteen in all, to send to a place of safety, when we heard on the radio the swathe of excitement caused by a black teenager who had stolen a car on the Berea, avoided police vans by driving the wrong way down one-way streets, and colliding with one of them, finally speeding down to the beachfront and crashing into four parked cars near us before running. A description of his clothing came over the air. Bernard jumped around to look back. "That's him: he's just walked past us." So he sprinted, and

I ran, silently. Bernard crash-tackled him outside a Wimpey Bar and I dropped on my knees on his back to cuff him, all within an arm's length of the nearest tables. A lot of interested diners and staff popped out to enquire. When told why, concern melted into enthusiastic approval.

The four or five vehicle crews who'd been in pursuit were a trifle nonplussed when we dragged him back to the crash scene to have him identified.

Perhaps the most strangely satisfied member of the public was a bloke who became an assistant manager of a hotel. He insisted on inviting me in for a drink and to meet his friends. I was cheerfully introduced as the cop who had arrested him fifteen minutes after he had reached Durban, for drunken driving.

Chapter 6

THE CITY POLICE

The City Police was the original police force in Durban. The town was founded in a formal sense in 1833 by a couple of dozen elephant hunters and traders who had established themselves at the Bay of Natal, which was then a large lagoon fringed in part by mangroves, with a bar across the entrance that allowed only intermittent tidal access to not very large ships. The primary attractions were the wildlife, particularly elephant and hippo, and the trading opportunities with the Zulu kingdom. Apparently, the very first town planning meeting consisted of an ox wagon carrying some barrels of beer and several local worthies while the rest rode horses. They set out the half-dozen or so main streets in the current central business district and made extensive land grants to the churches, but put them about thirty miles and a few rivers away. Next, they named the new town D'Urban, after the then governor of the Cape Colony. He totally ignored them, save to say that they were on their own in the wilds of Africa. Things changed when the emigrant Boers arrived after the Great Trek of 1838 and set up the Republic of Natalia, which the British soon felt themselves obliged to conquer and colonise.

The force was raised in about 1850 by the infant borough under the name of the Durban Borough Police, but initially served more as security guards, jail warders and process servers rather than police in the modern sense. By, say, 1875 they had evolved into a real force with discipline, uniforms and later a superintendent on a white horse. He had the difficult tasks of controlling the Gandhi riots in 1896, when the Mahatma was very nearly lynched, but smuggled out of the police station in disguise; and the dramas of the various wars.

In those days the borough was tiny compared with the Durban metropolitan area, which in the 1990s was a semicircle with a radius of some 40kms, with a population equal to New Zealand that is 3 000 000 or more. D'Urban then stretched from the top of the Berea to the sea, including the harbour (then only at the Point), Congella, and Greyville, running about four miles from north to south but not reaching the Umgeni or Umbilo rivers. It had a few thousand inhabitants. Stamford Hill, Sydenham and South Coast Junction (now Mobeni) were separate villages. Both rivers had hippos, which were royal game, until the mid to late 1800s, though the last elephant was shot on the Berea in about 1856. My mother remembered duiker running wild in Currie Road in about 1914.

By 1910 the police had a rather impressive headquarters next the town hall. It was three storeys high, had a gymnasium, and stables, cells, and armouries at the rear enclosing a parade ground. Now nothing of this is left. The site is occupied by Medwood Gardens. There were also some out stations, but of these I think only one building, much changed, still exists in different use. The police had both mounted units and a detective branch.

In the old Colony of Natal there were four police forces: the borough forces of Durban, Pietermaritzburg and Ladysmith, all modelled on English lines; and the Natal Mounted Police, a mounted paramilitary force which covered everything else, and in places had their own forts (as at Estcourt or Fort Nottingham). That was because Zululand to the north only came under British colonial control in 1887, and was later incorporated into Natal at the end of 1897. Pondoland to the south was annexed in 1896 by the Cape Colony. The old hotel in Harding, some five km from the Pondo border, was built in a square around a courtyard and in my time still had loopholes in the outer walls of the rooms. Basutoland, across the Drakensberg, became a British protectorate in 1881 after a campaign by Cape colonial forces. For good measure, the Boer republics of the Transvaal, Orange Free State, and from 1884 to 1888 the New Republic, lay to the west. Natal forces including the NMP fought four wars: the Zulu of 1879, the first and second Boer or Freedom wars of 1881 and 1899-1902, and the Bambata rebellion of 1906, which was the first ever fought by a British colony without imperial troops. This was done to prevent British political or military control of the campaign.

Before this, in 1845 British troops invaded the Boer republic of Natalia, establishing the old fort (now on Old Fort Rd) between the bay and the vlei, where they were promptly besieged. An unhappy ensign Prior perished there, and his cairn stood on the side of the road. The graves of those dozen or so killed in the Battle of Congella were nearby. Congella was not one of the best-thought-through battles: the British marched bravely up the beach and were shot up by Boers concealed in the mangroves.

After Union, all the various police forces carried on till 1914, when the SA Police was founded. The NMP became one of the four battalions of the SA Mounted Police, but the borough forces continued. Initially the SAP was very much an English-speaking force with many Boer War veterans, but the effect of the First World War was the loss of many and their replacement with Afrikaners, who dominated from some point in the 1920s.

In time, the Ladysmith force disappeared, while the Maritzburg one changed into a traffic police. The Durban force carried on uniquely as a police force, with formal recognition in statute as policemen not peace officers. The latter are law enforcement officers such as traffic police, park rangers, and even market masters, each with limited jurisdiction in the laws and areas they work. In the period to 1924 there was a strongly and widely expressed view in Durban that the SAP should stay out of town. After a lot of debate, the SA government appointed a divisional commissioner for Natal and directed him to set up shop in Durban. He arrived incognito, scouted the town, picked out various buildings to be stations, bought them, then staffed them. Hello Durban. While Central was already a government building, Berea and Umbilo were houses, Point a boarding house, and Somtseu Road possibly a warehouse or workshop.

The City Police went into a decline, lost its detectives, mounted unit, cells and all its old stations. I believe they were nearly abolished in the 1930s but lingered on till a new station building was built in about 1950 off Old Fort Road, when they got a fresh injection of support.

For many years they basically acted as traffic cops, but by the late 1970s they started to recover their ambition to be a real police force. Through the 1980s, two factions among them and the Council fought it out. Finally spurred on by the worsening crime and security situation in the early 1990's the Council found the necessary funds to enlarge the force with a new station at Phoenix, new radio systems and a Dog Unit. The SAP station at Phoenix had been established when it was a rural area of Indian smallholdings, and had not been greatly enlarged since. Gandhi established his Phoenix settlement there, with an ashram and a printing press. He also left his family behind there when he went off to save India. The settlement was burned down and destroyed by Zulu rioters in 1976. Prior to that, the City Council had built major townships for over 50 000 Indians on the old farmland, moving many from the old Tin Town areas on the flood plain of the Umgeni which had been pretty rough and crime-prone. The SAP, with a complement of perhaps 150, had simply been overwhelmed.

The City Police still had a chief constable, inspectors and

other English touches. They did not run any cells or a detective branch and still took the primary responsibility for traffic. Both forces now thought the other to be a friendly operation. From the 1950s to the 1970s, there had been a lot of ill feeling, partly as the City force was English-speaking and the SAP very much Afrikaans – and thus political and social opponents. This led to one notorious incident where two SAPs rushing to a complaint were arrested and handcuffed for speeding. Happily my arrival more or less coincided with their ambitious types with whom I worked happily, as, for instance, when I controlled the stands at the national rugby club championship while their man controlled the access roads. In time, after several collaborations and beers shared, he became assistant chief constable Gaffney and I a captain. Another of theirs was one Van der Merwe who became their inspector for Durban North.

I used their experts to give lectures on fake ID documents, driving licenses and currency notes, as they had many examples and could demonstrate how best to spot them.

In the streets they were reckoned the soft force but we were the hard slightly mad bastards who could and would shoot. This was at times very useful – saved a lot of hassles.

Chapter 7

HAPPINESS IS POINT CHARGE OFFICE

It may be helpful to describe Point's premises. The building was originally a two-storey boarding house with wide, red, concrete verandas on both floors along the street façade, built probably about 1900 when vaguely Italian columns were a popular ornament for a façade. Something of the old garden still hung on in front of the building but the back had been taken up by brick outbuildings and tarmac. These included a cell block, by then condemned and used for storage. In the 1980s a security wall and gateway, three metres high and of brick topped with razor wire, was built along the street boundary to discourage armed attacks. The Charge Office was to the left at ground level, with an entrance next the entry gate, and another doorway from the verandah about one and a half metres above the floor giving onto a flight of stairs leading down, which created a little walled landing like a pulpit overlooking the floor. This my daughter used to watch the action but to stay well out of it on her occasional visits there. To the rear of the Charge Office was a holding cell that could at a pinch take twenty or so people awaiting transport to the cell blocks at the Square or elsewhere. Next to that was a safe that served as an armoury. The room was divided roughly in half by a counter of brick topped with a 10cm thick slab of teak. There were stairs from the gate up to the main ground floor veranda where the station commander had his office and there was a lecture room.

Shifts generally paraded on there. More offices were upstairs while the CID had the rear extension. The whole place was rather run down and knocked about, with a slight sheen of condensation on the gloss-painted walls. The holding cell, and to a lesser extent, the Charge Office smelled of old grime and sweat with an overlay of disinfectant.

Across the road lay the rear of Addington, the big general and teaching hospital with tower blocks for the wards and the nurses' home, which fronted onto the beach. Along the beach was a strip of upmarket flats and hotels between six and twenty storeys high, but inland and to the south of that things went down rapidly to a working seaport level of oldish two-storey shops and housing mixed with warehouses and commercial properties running alongside the railway lines and docks down to the actual Point. This was where the main dock gates had been built in the early 1900s to admit the passengers for the old Union-Castle boats down about A to D shed. In about 1960, a new passenger terminal was built at T jetty to deal with liners and cold-storage cargoes, with a new entrance from the bottom of the Esplanade. Shepstone Road, that ran along the railway perimeter, was still a seriously rutted dirt road known as Point Airport, as it was easy for a van to take off. Poor White people lived down the Point, often in pretty stunted rooms in very modest flats, which rent control had made sure received very little maintenance. Anyone who thinks that the Whites were all rich is far from the mark. Someone once calculated that if you took the net worth of all the Whites in SA and gave it to the Blacks they would on average each get the price of a cinema ticket and a hamburger. Not for nothing was the Afrikaans nickname for rich suburbs *skuldbult* or debt hill. Point was a lively place with a longstanding reputation as the red light district and crime centre of the inner city.

The Charge Office at Point was the focal point for all the

dramas down that way so here is a sample of those days, and nights.

*

It was a hectic night at the Charge Office. The holding cell was full. There was a queue of arrestees to be charged and finger-printed. The drunks were noisy. Three men had been made to sit for want of space under the counter a solid old slab of hardwood.

Into this maelstrom came two genteel old white ladies. As I was briefly free and the most suitable member, I went to help. They wanted to report a minor traffic accident, that is, one without casualties. I got the form and we started. One of the three men under the counter, clearly drunk, suddenly jumped up and started shouting very loudly in Zulu about ten feet from us, making discussion wholly impossible. I mouthed "Excuse me" to the ladies and walked around a table to him.

"Shut up and sit down!" No reaction.

"I'm now asking you nicely to shut up and sit down." Still no reaction.

"OK, I'm now telling you to shut up and sit down."

More shouting so I put a hand on his shoulder and kicked his feet out from under him. He sat rather fast.

"Sorry about that," I said getting back to the ladies, "the station is rather busy tonight." We carried on. Sure enough the shouter jumps up: a repeat; he sits quietly again. We carry on.

Up he jumps again. Same sequence, except that this time the back of his head hits the counter on the way down with a big thud. "Sorry," to the ladies, "but some of these people need such a lot of persuasion."

We finished the form in peace. They then fled.

*

Another night I was lumbered with the job of reporting officer. I had to compile the hour by hour arrest figures for a nationwide crime blitz with numbers being phoned through to Area HQ.

At 0100 I was asked if we were, like other stations, ending off. "No, it's been quiet tonight but it'll pick up."

At 0300 I had to shout over the din to report the 17 arrests made since 0200 with more pending. Area had to stay open to 0400 just for us.

*

Someone arrested Leonardo for drunk in a public place: Leonardo the Teenage Mutant Ninja Turtle. He was a slight short Indian in his twenties in full kit: turtle shell, sword, headband, the lot. He was distressingly bouncy and voluble even in the holding cell – until he annoyed a cellmate. We heard a solid double thump and Leonardo suddenly went quiet. We found him lying at the foot of the wall. It turned out he'd irritated a kickboxer with a hangover.

*

I strolled into the Charge Office. Tussie was charging some guy who was complaining of being arrested "for naathing". Tussie sees me, says to the man: "He's an officer. He can explain it to you."

"Hey chief, they're wanting to lock me up for naathing."

"Mmm," I reply, not breaking stride. "You'd better be careful. Here you can get seven years for naathing."

The standard line of defence by Blacks arrested on the street was: "I was on my way to the cafe for a milk and a bread, when all of a sudden and for no reason some police started beating me and brought me here for naathing."

Another night, an arrestee was complaining he wanted an attorney. Tussie indicated me, that day in uniform, and said "You're in luck – he's an attorney."

The man gives me a careful but dirty look: "He's not a *!)&* attorney *se voet*." [He's not an attorney's foot.]

He wholly failed to understand why we all fell about laughing.

*

Once on the way back from a shoot some of us, dirty and dressed of course in overalls and scrap clothes in the back of a police truck, caused a certain amount of chaos at the traffic lights by pleading with the people in the adjacent cars to let us out as we had been locked up for nothing.

*

One of our new recruits spent four hours in that Charge Office and fled never to return. Ironically a few months later he was killed in a car crash two blocks away.

*

One sunny Saturday afternoon at 1330 I took over the station from a regular W/O Ndlovu for the afternoon shift. We checked the cash, the firearms, the books and all the rest, chatting and cracking the odd joke while signing over. He was a big jovial guy. He was off to drink a few beers and watch the soccer on TV. He had a good laugh at the thought of me spending my afternoon and evening on the Point populace.

By 1500 he was dead: six bullets in the back for his service pistol at the railway station. He was the last black member to travel to work in uniform.

*

One of my earlier encounters with Point Charge Office took place when the grill cell was inside the public side of the counter on the non-white side. Three of us from the Square were about to put a prisoner in, when a noisy fight started in the grill with a shout of "Knife!". We charged in with a Point man to break it up. This proved tricky, as we were slipping and sliding on the fresh blood on the floor. As the knife fell, I stooped to grab it. The knifeman tried to tackle me but one of my Indian colleagues hit him with a flat *klap*, that is, an open-handed slap, that started at the knee and hit him in the face, knocking him off his feet into the back wall.

*

One Saturday afternoon while working on the beachfront we heard a report of some White guy threatening people with a sword. I went down with a van to find a couple of our foot patrol had identified him and a couple of mates. He was carrying a metre-long homemade blade shaped a bit like a cutlass, tucked down the leg of his jeans. It turned out the three of them were from Port Elizabeth and could best be described as White *skollies*. The swordsman went in the grille. The really weird part was watching him talking to his mates. They were seriously inarticulate in both English and Afrikaans, speaking a jumble of words and phrases in a *tang* accent mixed with grunts and other odd noises while they continually touched their fingertips together through the mesh of the grille.

*

On busy nights when everyone was busy writing dockets, if someone started shouting he'd get a shout of *thula wena*/bly *stil*/shaddup from everyone, without anyone either pausing or looking up.

*

One night I came in to find a slosh of blood on the side wall about twelve feet above ground level. "What on earth is that? Clean it off."

"But what with?"

"Use your initiative – throw a prisoner at it."

*

The normal turnover of cases opened in Point was from 1,500 to 2,000 per month, an average of one every 15 or 20 minutes.

Arrests were at least as many. As far as I know, the only station in Natal busier than us was the Square. The arrests made each month by Reserve members ranged from say 50 to 80 but, exceptionally, as high as 150. Of those between a third and a half were first-schedule offences, the more serious ones – equivalent, I guess, to felonies. This meant Point routinely made more arrests than whole districts of reservists, and was probably the most active unit in Natal. Mind you, with a strength of about 50 members and a willing populace, it wasn't too hard. It also explains why both reservists and regulars reckoned their time there was arguably the most interesting of their career, certainly the most likely to evoke nostalgia.

One evening I arrived at about 1900 to find the troops complaining how quiet it was, how boring. They had been there for at least an hour without an arrest. I strolled out the gate, leaned on the wall, chatted to the gate guard, and waited. After ten minutes a drunk walked up to me. I arrested him and told the mothers' meeting to get out and do better.

*

I dropped by one sunny Saturday afternoon. Everything was very quiet. The complaints van had stopped by for a chat with the Charge Office people and a trio of reservists. Suddenly a radio call came through for an armed robbery in progress at the Ark Royal Cafe about a block away. The van crew ran for their van while everyone else bar the Charge Office sergeant ran straight out towards the cafe. As I neared the cafe it occurred to me that I was not on duty and was unarmed, so I slowed down. The alarm proved false.

*

Country stations could be quiet. Oliviershoek up in the Berg on the Ladysmith to Harrismith road reckoned to have four cases a month: one murder, one stock theft, and two traffic.

Their patrol van always carried a rifle and a shotgun; the first for buck, the second for guineafowl.

*

Another interesting statistic was the rate of arrest. Only once did I bother to calculate the rate of one of my members. Jones had been with us at Point nearly a year from first recruitment, one of our keen and bright youngsters at the Tech. He now was off to study airframe mechanics in Kempton Park so he asked if I could help him join the Flying Squad reserve unit up there. He had averaged about 70 hours a month with an arrest every 11 hours. I phoned the officer in charge to ask if he'd like to have him and told him his record. His response was "Is he your best man?" to which I replied after a little thought, "No, but he is one of our better new guys." The envy fairly boiled out of the earpiece.

A few weeks later I happened to mention this to our regular District Officer over a beer. He too was impressed. He remarked that the members of the regular beachfront patrol at the Square were averaging one arrest for every 192 hours worked, that is about one arrest each every five weeks. The worst though was an Umbilo squad created to tackle crime in the hospital car parks at King Edward and the San where many thefts of or out of cars took place. In their first eight weeks the twelve of them made no arrests, not even for drunk. Suddenly some of the causes for the resentment some regulars had towards reservists became very clear.

*

One fine night a woman was brought in to the Charge Office by a friend who was a nurse. She looked quite impressive as the whole of the left-hand side of her face, neck and shoulder was bruised blue. She seemed to be concussed; certainly she couldn't count fingers. It seemed her husband had been hitting her with a doorstop, a rock the size of a largish cabbage. Normal practice was for someone in this condition to be put in hospital overnight for observation in case of bleeding on the brain. She refused that, but was eventually persuaded to go to her friend for the night. A detailed entry was made in the occurrence book as a precaution. As it seemed the husband might be a dagga smoker, I went with Andrew Bertolotti to check up at the flat, found nothing, but had a brisk talk to the drunken husband.

A few weeks later at about 10 am on a Sunday Bertolotti and I were sent to an address by radio. We thought it familiar but couldn't place it till we got to the door to find this same couple. All four of us cried out, "Oh not you two again!" He was drinking brandy; she was drinking a cream liqueur; while her teenage daughter sniggered at his reactions to her mother's taunts. A happy family; and to cap it these lovebirds had been married four months.

*

There wasn't much sporting activity within the police, largely because everyone was on shifts or too busy to attend practices and matches. Occasionally there would be a family sports day for some of the stations at the lawns behind the barracks at the Square. On one day Point won the tug of war. For this I can claim some credit as anchor man, as I wound the tail of the rope around a tree. Absurdly, no one spotted this so the joke became official.

*

We'd arrested the Black female cashier at one of our less inspiring restaurants for illegal liquor selling. Over time I arrested every one of their staff for various offences. We took her back to the station with all the dozen or two beers seized. Godfrey and I were writing the paperwork at the table in the Charge Office with the cashier sitting opposite us and the cans lined up between us sorted for inventory. In came a strange, middle-aged White guy, podgy, dressed in a security guard's uniform with a gold-braided soft-peaked cap perched on top of his bush of curly fair hair. He claimed the beers belonged to him and were being looked after for him.

"So these beers are yours?"

"Yes."

"So they will know you?"

"Unnh, yes."

"So if you call them they will go to you?"

"Unnh, what?"

"OK would you care to call them?"

At this he looked wildly at us, both wholly serious, and the cashier, who had her hand over her mouth, and fled. Genteel applause ran around the Charge Office.

Chapter 8

WHORES

We had at Point a curious relationship with the street whores, the massage parlour whores, and, to a lesser extent, with the ship whores (but the latter largely operated outside our area, save for a couple of night clubs they frequented). We would occasionally arrest them for solicitation or loitering, but they treated this as income tax. If there was a dangerous criminal around they were first at risk so they would give information, generally on the basis that they'd never give evidence in court. I once helped arrest a wanted murderer in a pool room in a cafe used by their pimps. If we wanted to get information in a hurry, we might buy bunny chows and cool drinks and a magazine; park in their area, turn on the blue light, and eat and read very slowly. Don Vermoter reckoned he could take two minutes to read a page of a photoromance. Many of them we knew by name and repute. Their pimps, though, we neither knew nor cared much for.

*

We were in our happy yellow car, stopped at a robot near Point Road. Next to us was a white guy in his car, with, next to him, a black woman arrayed in short dreadlocks and a scarlet mock-velvet dress with a cleavage to her navel secured by lace that looked like chicken wire – odd, but not an offence. He noticed our interest, panicked and drove off straight through three red robots. We pursued, right up to the eighth floor of a parking garage where he ran out of space.

Back at Point Charge Office, we booked him for the various traffic offences. She started shouting and screaming and would not stop till she was taken outside and gassed. It turned out he had a wife and two tiny kids at home and was a bank manager. My sergeant, like him Afrikaans, gave him a brutally graphic lecture on disease, death and morality. He left stepping over his temporary girlfriend who was lying head-down, coughing, on the stair.

*

One take-over evening at Point, my sergeant, Athalie Bauer, was anxious to get her complaints van on the road at once. She grabbed the first two to arrive in uniform, so I found myself driving with a new guy just transferred in that week. We were given a stabbing complaint. We drove to the place and stopped.

"There's no one here," says the new man. "It must be false."

"Naah, stick around, something will happen."

Sure enough, up ran a pimp to say they'd chased the knifeman and had him cornered behind a nearby block of flats. The back yard was concreted, with six-inch-deep water furrows crossing it. The man was in the servants' quarters. There was an eight-foot concrete wall to our left, the brick building to our right, about six feet apart with a diagonal furrow. We shouted to him to come out. He did, but with knife in hand. We covered him with our pistols, told him to put the knife down. He did not. He came forward with his knife levelled at us. My colleague knocked his knife hand down. I grabbed him and ran him head first into a wall before cuffing him. Then we had the problem of keeping the pack of pimps and others off him. They were armed with lengths of reinforcing rod, bits of 2x4, even a no 7 iron and a spear, all trying to hit him on the head and shoulders as we hustled him up and down some steps and into the van.

I then asked where the complainant was.

"No, she's with a client," says her pimp.

"How long'll she be?"

"About thirty or forty minutes."

"OK, no statement from her, no charge. Get her to the Charge Office or he walks."

She arrived as promised, with a fairly deep wound in the top of her left shoulder. She'd had it stitched and bandaged at Casualty at Addington, then gone straight back to work. As the bandage was disarranged, I had one of my members – a paramedic – rebandage her while we took her statement at the counter.

*

John Walters and I agreed one evening at an officers' meeting in Boland House to go have pizza on the beachfront. We were in our work clothes so looking quite respectable, if not lahnie. Parking was a problem so I strolled towards our rendezvous. A short, greasy Indian approached me to enquire if I wanted company, which he appeared able and most willing to supply. I replied noncommittally. As we neared John, I pointed him out to my new best friend, and fell back a pace to mouth "pimp" to John. He caught on at once and used his best Kent accent. We then passed ourselves off as a couple of British businessmen on a visit to SA. Then came the negotiations. Our friend tried hard to wangle taxi fare and other upfront cash payments out of us. John countered with a series of incentives and performance-related bonuses, claiming knowledge of similar arrangements in King's Cross, Sydney and Singapore. When asked where we were staying I named a hotel I'd just walked past. We even started arguing about our room numbers. We agreed to meet him and the girls in the foyer of that hotel.

To make charges of pimping or solicitation stick, we had to agree a cash price with them – which can be tricky. The night manager watched us wander into the foyer. Once the pimp and his girls arrived, we made a distinctly suspicious group. We sat chatting. His suspicions rose. He clearly didn't fancy his hotel being used as a knocking shop. As he started towards us with two security guards, John finally managed to fix the prices with all three. I pulled my police ID and arrested them, cheerfully helped by the securities, who took them out back to a store room. John phoned Radio for a van. While we waited, our friend offered us a deal. If we let them go, he'd let us have his A team for free, not this B team.

Four months later at the trial, John was vastly embarrassed to find his choice, the prettier one, now very obviously pregnant.

*

Kathy van Zyl was the so-called doyenne of the street whores. She was probably the oldest being a grandmother. Her daughter was a data processor in Westville with two little girls. I once asked Kathy why she didn't retire, get a job with her daughter, and take it easy. She said she was used to the life and wouldn't settle.

I first met her one night when I was cruising with Bertolotti on crime prevention. We noticed a couple of men trying to start a car just off Fisher Street. As this could have been a theft, we stopped a couple of blocks away and I walked forward a block to take a closer look. While I watched, a stout middle-aged whore asked me if I wanted some company. I declined as I was still watching. She wandered off, but just as I decided the car people were all right, Kathy came asking. I started an unenthusiastic negotiation with her until she named the price. It must have been a quiet night. I fumbled in my shirt pocket as if for money, pulled my ID and grabbed her. Pimps and whores came for me, but so did my back-up, at speed. That stopped the opposition. We bundled her into the car where she promptly wet herself, much to the disgust of Bertolotti who had to clean the car. He even had to go back to get her some dry clothes. She was most embarrassed to have solicited a local cop – especially an officer. Afterwards we got quite friendly and I would stop for the occasional chat.

*

Ironically the two streets, Fisher and Pickering, that were the centre of the street whores' area were named after two eminently respectable Methodist town councillors of the late 1800s.

*

If you think whores are pretty, you either could afford the call girls proper at R2 000 a night or you've never seen a street whore. Few had looks of any note. One of the more notable in the Fisher Street area was called Tugboat, which described her well, barring the squint in her left eye. One of the less appealing women was a hard-faced Indian who was reputedly a specialist in the blow job. She looked as if she earned her living biting the heads off live rats. In those days the going rate – at least for locals – was R60 to R80 for forty-five minutes. A hand job was cheapest, the other two standards were more. More advanced stuff like chains and leather, transgenders and fetishism was handled by a few specialists who worked out of clubs or massage parlours rather than the street. The massage parlours tended to have girls who could be mistaken for typists, and cubicles you could kick to pieces in a couple of minutes. I once listened with amusement to one parlour owner giving a verbal job reference on one of her girls to another owner. Barring a couple of small items it was stunningly normal.

*

There was one solitary street girl who'd been at a decent school, Westville Girls High. She must have volunteered as her prospects elsewhere must have been far better. At first she looked quite pretty and dressed well, but after a couple of years her eye was dulled, and her skin looked rather like blotting paper and was prone to rashes or pimples – all signs of drug addiction.

*

Our estimate was that at least 70% of the street whores were on drugs, and about half were lesbians. They presumably didn't want to mix business with pleasure. Virgins attracted a premium rate, but they never lasted more than three months. Most White recruits seemed to be teenage runaways from rural places like Lichtenburg, heading for the bright lights but then effectively kidnapped by pimps who fed them drugs till they became addicted. The pimps were, in general, an uninspiring crew dressed cheaply and messily – the food-stained windcheater was popular. They played a lot of pool and tended to hunt in packs. Oddly, the street whores were nearly all White, though their pimps quite often were Indian. Massage parlour and ship whores were a mixture; the latter included Blacks who went directly on board ships. Some effectively acted as local wives to two or three ship's officers. My mother believed one lived in her block in Morningside.

*

Quixotic as it may seem, I did once open a kidnap and assault docket for two massage parlour girls. They were two Indian girls, about nineteen years old. A White man took them off to a hotel at the far end of Umbilo, but then held them at gunpoint for some hours.

*

Our attention was drawn to one Black whore down Alice Street. She was exchanging insults with a bunch of guys in a car and pelting them with cooldrink cans. She was drunk but annoyed because she had diagonal razor slashes across her back from shoulder to hip, about a hundred stitches worth.

*

Rock-bottom of the whores were the truck-stop lot. All Black, they operated at the main truck park at the back of North Beach where long-distance trucks stayed overnight. They reputedly charged R10 on a dry night but R5 when it rained. Trucks ran from Durban north as far as Congo, Kenya and Uganda, stopping for safety in similar truck stops all over. This was one of the main methods for the spread of Aids from its original source somewhere around the Great Lakes.

*

We did of course have rent boys too. They tended to operate from shop entrances in the CBD. I was walking my mother from the theatre to my parking garage late one evening when she asked why all these Indian boys were hanging around so late. She was most surprised.

*

An occasional tactic was the decoy. Here, the whore chats up the man and takes him to her flat. On the way a couple of thugs rob him at knifepoint while she vanishes.

*

An odd case involving a whore took place one night. A highly annoyed citizen turned up shagged-out but penniless. He had had the service then gone naked to the bathroom. Once inside, he found the door shut and no handles on the door. He therefore climbed out the window and, because he was on the third floor, clung by his toes and fingertips to the very thin ledges on the facade. He managed to reach the bedroom window and climb back in. There he found his wallet had been stripped of his month's wages. The whore was known to the regulars at Point as a reputable type, who hung out at the Monte Carlo night club. I went there with a couple of City Police types who refused to go in with me but stayed outside at the bottom of the stairs. I was immediately welcomed by an assistant manager who found her. Back at Point, she admitted everything but the theft of the money. I later heard that a man had been arrested in Port Elizabeth for this and several similar thefts. He spotted men going with whores, followed them, then slid in at a convenient moment to lift their cash.

*

One evening Matthew Dunstan and I were strolling past a seedy restaurant when I heard the outside man ask me: "Want a steak? Want a woman?" I was surprised as I'd arrested staff there before, but I backed up and enquired. After some discussion he took us a couple of blocks north into the Square's area where his women were in a parked car. We agreed price and venue, which was to be in a nearby flat. When we seized them for the arrest they started screaming and we were attacked by three Indian guys who we took for pimps. A brisk brawl started until I pulled my ID to arrest them, only to find they were Vice Squad members from the Square. We all then turned around and grabbed the pimp and his merchandise.

*

The snappiest dresser on the street for a couple of years, specialising in little black dresses and large cosmetic belt buckles, was a Coloured called Eric. He used to get wildly indignant if we stopped off while he was chatting up a prospect, calling out stuff like: "Howsit going Eric my man?"

*

Another Coloured character – a real woman this time – used to operate at the top end of Pine Street. She stood next to an arcade and flagged down Mercedes and Jaguars heading for the Western Freeway. She'd cut a deal with an up-front payment to hire an upstairs room for the frolic, then blow him a kiss and go into the arcade which turned left into the cross-street where her car was parked. There she'd change her wig and clothes, alter her make up, then stroll back around the street corner. The sucker as a rule gave up and left, but she managed on occasion to commiserate with him, and take another advance.

*

One of our smaller Coloured members, Alvin Geschwindt, won a novel distinction. He alone was chased a full block by a transsexual whore beating him over the head with her stiletto heel. He was most aggrieved at our laughter. He reckoned it was bloody sore.

*

Occasionally in my earlier days in Point, we staged decoy street whores. A couple of our female members, Athalie, who was the blonde, and Leslie Marais, who had black hair, were quite keen on this adventure so they tarted themselves up and took up stances at the bottom of the Esplanade, near but slightly off the real whores' pitches. We didn't need attacks from their pimps. It worked quite well and they pulled several punters. What intrigued me was how competitive it became between them. We dropped this after a while, largely because we needed two vehicles and at least six men to cover them against assault or kidnap.

*

One of the more revolting incidents took place at a whore's flat that we raided on information of dagga and mandrax. As usual, there was a steel mesh door so we had to knock, listen to the toilet flush and then go in. Inside was a youngish White whore with her Indian pimp plus his pal. The kitchen was spectacularly filthy: a drift of rubbish spread from the floor up over the top of the counters. Most of the furniture consisted of ashtrays. She suddenly became rather agitated, showing considerable discomfort around the groin. I suggested she go to the bathroom to sort herself out, but sent a female member, who'd been outside, in with her. It turned out she'd shoved three mandrax tablets up her vagina with a still wrapped tampax to keep them up. It was the sharp edges of the plastic doing the damage. A chemist later told me that the effect of the mandrax would have been wild had it stayed there long, as any absorbed there would have gone directly to the brain without any passage through the kidneys. Our girl, not yet hardened to the ways of the world, didn't manage to stop her flushing them away. We searched the place thoroughly, opening sockets, inspection hatches and other possible hidey-holes. We found enough dagga seeds and stubs and silver foil filters from zol cigarettes to make arrests. The bad bit was the nappy bucket. She said she had a young baby that she boarded with a friend. From about six down the nappies were crawling with maggots.

1 (above) The old Central Police Station. The Charge Office was on the ground floor on the right. This is a late colonial building, of a modest functional type.

2 (below) The new Magistrates' Courts and C.R. Swart Square. The podium held the civil and most of the district courts, the tower block the regional courts. The Square is to its right; both were on part of the old Stamford Hill airfield, which was originally a vlei.

3 (above) View of Central Durban and the Esplanade. The Town Hall, which is a duplicate of Belfast's, and the Post Office are to the lower right. This was part of the old Central's area. The Esplanade runs along the bayside towards Congella, where the ships and sugar terminal are to be found.

4 (below) City Centre in about 1910, presumably in the rush hour. The old City Police HQ is the red brick building above the tram. The Town Hall is on the left. The Post Office, which had been the Town Hall, has the tallest tower.

5 (above) Point Police Station. The Charge Office was behind the small square windows to the left. The shrubs are new, and the razor wire has gone since my time.

6 (below) View of Point and the Bluff. This shows the whole of Point's area, which has since been largely built up. The stadium at bottom left is Kingsmead Cricket Ground. The rugby and soccer stadia were further north.

7 (above) Dock Gates in the 1920s/1930s. The gates and nearly all the buildings were still there in my time, but now most of this is tower blocks.

8 (below) Addington hospital when new. Casualty is on the right; the tower block was wards.

9 (above) 1970s beach scene looking from North Beach to South and Addington Beaches, when these were designated for Whites only. Beaches designated for Blacks and Indians were further north.

10 (below) 1990s beach scene near the paddling pools. The New Year and other busy days we policed on foot were like this, with perhaps 250,000 people in the area happily intent on a peaceful day out.

11 (above) Greyville Racecourse, probably on a July Handicap day. The members' ring was to the right, the gold and silver rings to the left. Picnics were in the centre, off left.

12 (left) My medals. On the left is one for ten years' faithful service. The initials "TD" above the lion stand for Troue Diens. The one on the right was merely for being a member on the 75th anniversary of the force in 1989, which in time served as a de facto long-service medal.

13 Award for 10 Year Medal, signed (nine years after the time had been served) by General Fivaz, the last head of the SAPS to retire peacefully. The badge is the new one, though it was unclear whether the aloe was chosen because it is notoriously bitter and often twisted.

Toekenning / Awarding

van 'n Ererang deur die Minister van Wet en Orde / **of an Honorary Rank by the Minister of Law and Order**

Aan / To: DOUGLAS NEAL WADE

Groete / Greetings

Aangesien ek besondere geloof en vertroue in u lojaliteit, moed en goeie gedrag het, en handelende op advies van die Kommissaris van die Suid-Afrikaanse Polisie, stel ek u aan, kragtens en behoudens die bepalings van regulasie 8 (1) van die Regulasies vir die Suid-Afrikaanse Reserwepolisiemag, soos afgekondig by Goewermentskennisgewing R.1016 in Buitengewone Staatskoerant 275 (Regulasiekoerant 93) van 29 Junie 1962 (soos gewysig, met die ererang van LUITENANT in die Suid-Afrikaanse Reserwepolisiemag met ingang van die 1 dag van OKTOBER 19 89

I, reposing special trust and confidence in your loyalty, courage and good conduct, and acting on the advice of the Commissioner of the South African Police, do, by virtue of and subject to the provisions of regulation 8 (1) of the Regulations of the South African Reserve Police Force, as promulgated under Government Notice R.1016 in Government Gazette (Extraordinary) 275 (Regulation Gazette 93) of 29 June 1962 (as amended), appoint you in the honorary rank of LIEUTENANT in the South African Reserve Police Force as from the 1 day of OCTOBER 19 89

U moet derhalwe u pligte nougeset en ywerig nakom in die ererang wat u nou beklee of in enige hoër ererang waartoe dit my of my opvolgers, op aanbeveling van die Kommissaris van die Suid-Afrikaanse Polisie van tyd tot tyd hierna mag behaag om u aan te stel of te bevorder, en moet u die lede van die Suid-Afrikaanse Reserwepolisiemag onder u bevel deeglik in al die werksaamhede van die Suid-Afrikaanse Reserwepolisiemag oplei en alles in u vermoë doen om doeltreffendheid, goeie orde en tug te handhaaf, en gebied ek dat hulle u, ooreenkomstig die bepalings van die Polisiewet, 1958 (Wet No. 7 van 1958), as hul meerdere moet gehoorsaam.

Verder gebied ek dat u enige bevele en opdragte wat u van tyd tot tyd van my, in bogenoemde hoedanigheid, of van enige van u meerderes mag ontvang, moet uitvoer ooreenkomstig bogenoemde Wet en enige Staande Orders uitgevaardig kragtens die Wet en alle ander Wette, Regulasies en Orders wat op die Suid-Afrikaanse Reserwepolisiemag betrekking het.

You shall therefore conscientiously discharge your duty in the honorary rank which you now hold or in any higher honorary rank to which I or my successors may from time to time, on the recommendation of the Commissioner of the South African Police, hereafter be pleased to promote you, and you shall train the members of the South African Reserve Police Force under your command in all the functions of the South African Reserve Police Force and do your utmost to promote efficiency, good order and discipline, and I command that they shall obey you, as their superior officer, in accordance with the provisions of the Police Act, 1958 (Act No. 7 of 1958).

I further command that you shall observe such orders and directions as from time to time you may receive from me, acting as aforesaid, or from any of your superiors in accordance with the aforesaid Act and any Standing Orders issued under the Act and all Acts, Regulations and Orders applicable to the South African Reserve Police Force.

Gegee onder my hand te / Given under my hand at PRETORIA

op hede die / this 14 dag van / day of APRIL 19 92

Minister van Wet en Orde: Republiek van Suid-Afrika
Minister of Law and Order: Republic of South Africa

14 Award of Honorary Commission, given on promotion to officer rank, i.e. to lieutenant. Signed not by the king, as was my father's naval commission, but by a minister. The badge is the original SAP type with the then South African coat of arms.

15 Reserve Candidate Officers' Course, 7 to 18 August 1989. In the front row, the centre three are Major J.J. Stumke (course leader), Colonel W. Grove (Commanding Officer advanced training, and later Lieutenant-General in charge of the CID) and Lieutenant H. Weitz (class officer). Non-White officers would have gone to the other colleges. By 1997 there were many Indian and a couple of Black reserve officers in Durban, of which the most senior was the Indian Major in charge of Chatsworth.

16 (upper left, opposite page) 1994 Election: Day 1. Standing: Captain D.N. Wade and Constable Roland Dunstan (both wearing summer uniform), Sergeant Don Vermoter, Constable Petty Naidoo and the others (all in field dress). Squatting: Constable Moonsamy, Constable Moorgas, Sergeant Nollie van Zyl and Warrant Officer Ian Thompson.

17 (lower left, opposite page) 1994 Election: Van Crew. Don Vermoter and me. This was a standard yellow van, slightly battered and weary, definitely not bullet proof, with enough rust on the body to prove it was a Durban van.

18 (above) 1994 Election: Parading On, Day 2. KZP Sundumbili. L to R: Constables Fuhri, Snyders, Lancaster and Van Buren Scheele making safe and loading.

19 (above) 1994 Election: Guard Unit, Isithebe School. L to R: a KwaZulu Police (KZP) member carrying a G3 rifle, Constable Snyders, another KZP member, Sergeant Godfrey Hamshire. The houses in the background are very ordinary township types.

20 (below) 1994 Election: Guard Unit, near Isithebe. L to R: Two KZP members, Constable Jones with standard shotgun, KZP, Constable Snyders carrying one of our shortened shotguns. The van is in KZP livery. Some of those were made bulletproof by mounting six-ply sheets of Kevlar inside the cab, which reduced every dimension by about 15 cm – very tight and airless.

Chapter 9

TRAINING

New recruits had to go through a series of lectures on the law, the police paperwork, and the practicalities of the job. When I started, these were done rather haphazardly during the monthly meetings. Recruits were supposed to be literate in English or Afrikaans, but in reality we had from semi-literates to graduates. English was used as the language of instruction, though questions could be asked and answered in Afrikaans. We had all races, all ages from 18 to 70, and all sexes.

I started giving lectures on a relatively informal basis when I was a constable at the Square. My initial promotion to sergeant was hurried up when someone noticed I was about to lecture at divisional level seminars with no rank. By about 1990, this evolved into a district training post which I held concurrently with being the branch commander at Point. I had two lecturers plus guests. Broadly speaking, Athalie Bauer dealt with the niceties of Charge Office paperwork, while Alan Christie from Berea, an assistant bank manager, handled weapons (theory and stripping), while I focused on the law. We used the lecture room up at Berea SAP as it was the most central in the district and we could use it without interruption.

The law focused on crimes against the person, crimes against property, traffic offences, and by-law offences.

Crimes against the person started with murder, then descended through culpable homicide to assault with intent to cause grievous bodily harm (normally called GBH), to common assault (which embraced assault by blowing cigarette smoke in someone's face) and more usefully assault by threat. One example was a shoplifter showing the pistol under his jacket to a shop assistant and saying quietly: "See you at the rank." Stab wounds in the throat, torso or groin would be taken as attempted murder. One useful procedural point was that an accused could always be found guilty of a lesser charge of a similar nature to that on the docket; so attempted murder could lead to a conviction for GBH, but not fraud or theft. Rape (which we thought of as more a form of assault than sex) and indecent assault were a subset that we often treated separately, together with paedophilia and the other exotica, such as the seduction of schoolboys by their form mistress, to be found in the Immorality Act.

My approach had to be simple and graphic. My test to distinguish murder from culpable homicide was this. If you arrive on the scene to find a dead body with someone standing over it saying: "Got the bastard!" that's murder; if he's saying "Oh shit." that's culpable homicide. We used to use our personal experiences to illustrate the practicalities, while asking them to remember the many people who had died or been crippled to enliven our talks.

Crimes against property concentrated on robbery, housebreaking, theft and fraud. Again we used common examples to define the distinction, say, between robbery, and theft by snatching. Here, a handbag snatch that pulled the woman to the ground or dragged her along was robbery. Housebreaking was a dual crime: housebreaking with intent to, say, steal, and theft. If the reason for the housebreaking was baffling, we could list it as "with intent to commit a crime unknown to the prosecutor". The smallest fraud was the switching of price tags on goods in supermarkets.

For traffic, we made sure that they knew how to handle

drunk driving and hit and run cases, as well as reckless or negligent driving, which we handled, but the minor technical stuff we left pretty much to the City Police.

The municipal by-laws had a wide range of minor nuisance offences, like fighting, disturbance, or obscene language – as well as my favourite, which I never had a chance to use, which stopped the brake blocks on an ox wagon from protruding more than three inches outside the wheel rims. Used intelligently, these gave you a lot of discretion to make arrests before things got out of hand.

We turned out three courses per year each of about thirty new recruits from District 46, which embraced Point, the Square or Central, Berea, Umbilo, Maydon Wharf, Montclair and Mayville. We also did specific one-off lectures for all members on topics such as rape, child protection or recognition of forged documents or money.

I used to open the first lecture by asking them: "Which of you are paranoid?" There would be a cautious pause but no volunteers.

"Well, if you don't become paranoid, you'll soon be dead."

This was one way to bring home the fact that the force countrywide was losing over 200 members a year murdered. It also weeded out the diffident. Happily, none of my trainees were ever – as far as I know – killed on duty, but one White member from the Square, a decent bloke, was stabbed to death at the Workshop shopping mall when he tried to break up a fight at the bar he was working at.

I also used to remind them, half-jokingly, that they could always arrest anyone they could see at any time. If he is standing on the pavement, arrest him for obstruction; if walking, for jostling and annoying other pedestrians; if lying down, for imitating a corpse in a public place; if breathing, for atmospheric pollution; if not breathing, for littering and refusing to remove litter; if crossing the road, for failing to cross fast enough. A colleague at Nottingham Road was thrilled when I told him of this offence – sec111(f) of the Road Traffic Ordinance – as he reckoned he could arrest the entire village at any time. If all else fails, pretend to be deaf, ask him the time and when he finally answers in a shout, arrest him for disturbance. Another one useful on occasion was the obscene gesture, for which there was no admission of guilt. With luck, if you smiled and waited a bit, someone swearing at you at, say, a cricket match would be fool enough to make a gesture at the police, who would promptly invite him in for the weekend.

All members were trained on pistols, hand machine carbines, HMCs, automatic shotguns and rifles. In my early days there were still some drophead Webleys and .38 revolvers in the armouries, but these were replaced first by Walther pistols with a six-round magazine and later by the Z88, a locally made large-frame pistol that carried a fifteen-round magazine. This was a solid reliable piece. When I was made up to lieutenant I was issued my own, which I had modified from a 4lb to a 1.5lb trigger pull to make the first shot easier and thus more accurate. Female members generally found this too big to hold, so they and men with small hands used small-frame 9mms or .32s.

HMCs fired .22 bullets in mags of thirty or fifty. If dropped, they could fire off a whole mag; they were also more prone to jamming than other arms. Personally I did not like them and never carried one, but enthusiasts reckoned they were great for indoor use, as in house penetration, when you could spray bullets down corridors using the ricochets.

The shotguns held seven rounds and were issued with a bandolier of forty rounds: some birdshot, some buckshot (which was used mainly against vehicles). If you were practised, you could feed rounds into the weapon while firing, so maintaining constant fire. Very effective at distances up to seventy to a hundred metres, this was the best heavy weapon for urban use, as overshoots or ricochets were not a problem.

Rifles were originally wooden-butt R1 models, heavy, unwieldy in vehicles, but very accurate with a flat trajectory for 400m. Later the R4 with a metal fold-up butt came in. With the butt folded, you could handle it like a huge pistol from a Terminator movie. They carried mags of twenty, thirty or fifty rounds, which frequently were taped together in pairs to help fast reloading – especially by the Dog Squad. I liked them, but at Point we did not use them for safety reasons. An overshoot could go far, possibly three or four km, while the bullets could bounce off walls, pavements, poles, even windows if the angle was shallow enough. I once saw a Mercedes with a sloping back windscreen which had deflected a dozen 9mm bullets, leaving only small copper smudges at the points of impact. The overshoot horror story of our days took place in Port Elizabeth, where a pregnant woman at a shopping centre was hit by an overshoot from a range three kms away, which killed her baby.

In my first five years or so, the training given was enthusiastic but rather fitful. A lot of the legal and paperwork teaching was given in the form of one- or two-day seminars held at various venues around Durban involving stations as far out as Umlazi, KwaMashu, and even Inanda, which were all Black. I can remember lecturing to audiences of a hundred or more through an interpreter, normally one of their senior NCOs. This made for a rather peculiar response. If I told a joke, some would laugh at once, others after the translation, and all of them at random times after the interpreter presumably made his own. In front of Indian classes, I felt at times like an English comic at the Glasgow Empire theatre. Gradually though, training was limited to individual districts, largely, I suspect, as budgets tightened and effort went into extra security. Big gatherings of unarmed uniformed reservists were too good a target.

Policemen must remember they are a service. If they cannot or will not do the job, the public go elsewhere. An example of this is the black vigilante groups that operated in some areas.

Training

In one case, in the Transvaal, a girl was gang-raped. She complained to the police and named the attackers. The police arrested them, but the court released them on bail the next day. The vigilantes thought this inadequate so they got her to point them out, then grabbed them and handcuffed them naked to a streetlight pole. They handed her a sjambok and invited her to flog them. They then flogged them nearly cripple, put a big notice on the pole to say what they had done, and left them overnight in a sub-zero winter wind. The moment the police will not or cannot go everywhere, a civil war has started.

I managed to push through written tests for recruits at the Square and, over quite a lot of opposition, for existing members. The simple problem was that we had no idea what they could do unless we had seen them doing the job. The classic case was an elderly White bloke, previously at Somtseu Road, who had been a member for six or eight years and had been made a sergeant. As he was about sixty, he spent his time in the Charge Office, yarning for hours. He would not and could not handle outside duties, so Lt Barker made him our catering sergeant, only to find he couldn't boil water or butter bread. When – after a lot of pressure – I got him to write a beginner's test, he scored 5%: by far the lowest, about 10% below a semi-literate. For all his hours, he was totally unable to carry out the simplest Charge Office tasks. It was so bad the lieutenant and I suppressed the result and destroyed the paper. Unabashed, he actually made a formal complaint when he wasn't promoted to a Warrant.

Mind you, these embarrassing types were around, promoted – according to rumour – as they sold cheap shirts, did free car services or donated meat for braais. R/Sgt Botha, an active and knowledgeable member, transferred from Point to George. There, one night he attended a motor collision. In the van was a local Warrant in the reserve. The sergeant hopped out to check for injuries and damage and take control of the scene. He asked the Warrant to divert traffic. After a bit he noticed nothing had happened. He went back to find the Warrant still sitting in the van because he didn't even know how to put out cones.

Weapons training, similarly, was rather hit and miss. Stripping and maintenance could be and was done at the station, but range days were problematic. There was no police range in Natal of any sort, not even a pistol range at the Square, so basically we had to go cap in hand to the army. They were happy to help, but of course after they had satisfied their own needs. I can recall travelling in convoys of police trucks to ranges down the South Coast, to the Bluff, to a range inland from Umzinto, up the North Coast to a lichee farm, and inland past Howick. Sometimes it was for a single day but, where possible, we made a weekend of it. There we would have, say, sixty rounds of 9mm at targets at five, seven and ten metres; twenty-five rounds with a rifle at hundred-metre targets; perhaps a clip of twenty on automatic fire; another clip on an HMC; and a few rounds of shotgun, where possible, at pop-up man-targets in a bush lane. The basic day's shooting took about 143 rounds.

If you need to disguise a firearm to defeat a ballistics expert, you can swap the barrel with another from a similar firearm. The frames are numbered but the barrels are not. Failing that, toss a pinch of very fine dust in the barrel and fire twenty rounds, or skip the dust and fire thirty reloads. But do lose the *doppies*.

Doppies can give excellent fingerprints even after firing – normally partials of the right thumb from the loading of the magazine.

We also had to experience tear gas. The first time I wore a gasmask, I stood in between three gas grenades – until I noticed the mask filters didn't work. The best way to recover was to stand still like a penguin with your face to the sun, as the gas was volatile and evaporated. Technically the gas was smoke but no one called it that. It could lie in the soil and be kicked up, so I have marched at the head of a singing platoon, between classes, down a dirt road, to find the tail choking and coughing with the gas. One of the funnier incidents was during a demonstration of a gas gun that fired gas canisters about seventy metres. The guys from the riot squad had set up ambushes on the bush path. A couple of canisters landed under a tree, releasing a cloud that went straight up. After a minute or so, John Walters – then a Warrant – tumbled down ten feet, coughing and cursing, something he very seldom did. The demonstrator, a Warrant from Umbilo, refused to say how that could possibly have happened.

To throw a hand grenade more than a hundred metres, take a plastic mug, two metres of string, and a grenade of your choice – but not one with a zero delay. Tie the ends of the string firmly to the top and bottom of the handle of the mug. Place the grenade in the mug with the lever inside the mug. Remove the safety pin. Hold the centre of the string and swing the mug around your head as fast as possible. Twitch the mug to release the grenade towards the target. Safety warning: do not do this indoors.

To fell a smallish tree in a hurry, wrap a length of cortex around the trunk and fire. For a trunk of fifteen cm diameter, two loops are needed.

If we stayed overnight, it was usually in tents and sleeping bags borrowed from the army. They weren't too bad. The real horror was the latrines, so-called "flying saucers" balanced precariously on railway lines over the pit. A very wooden spoon went to the first poor sod to fall in. Once we got to a site near Port Shepstone to find the promised tents had gone to the border, so we made a tent from canvas satchels buckled together and hung over a tree branch, which worked remarkably well. You could get a little hot water from the cooks for shaving, but bathing was in the river, with the ladies round a bend out of sight.

At some camps some over-keen types favoured the idea of night raids. Once this was seriously mooted. I was in a tent with other Warrants and some older sergeants. We let it be known that if anyone tried it on us we would roll off our camp beds and immediately open fire out of the tent. We were not disturbed. Over time I got to know nearly all the NCOs from the North and South Coasts, the far South Coast, Pinetown and Durban, and the officers from the whole province.

A few of the women went to camp to catch men. Torrid rumours of sex on the water tanker went around. One rather obvious bird took the trouble to limp with a bucket past a lecture class. We all watched in fascination but nobody said a word. On her way back – even more pathetic as she now had water in the bucket – she did get a response: "Hey you're limping on the wrong leg!" She stopped, thought, then limped off on the other leg.

I got the best recipe for *putu* from a Zulu cook on one camp. Add one part mashed potato for three or four parts mealie meal. It makes a moister, smoother mix and the *putu* has a nice mealie flavour, not the usual dry cardboard offering.

Luckily the problems around practical training were solved by the initiative and energy of Chris de Wet, a reservist at Tongaat. He worked for Tongaat Estates and noticed that there was an abandoned quarry on their land. He persuaded the directors to let him use that, plus some unused land in a steep river valley running past the quarry, as a range and camp site. Over the next few years, he built ranges for handguns, a serious bush path, a combat shooting range, and a big braai area, or *lapa*, next a couple of existing small buildings. The quarry did for a rifle range; there were cliffs for abseiling; space for lectures in marquees; and lots of parking. The Durban and North Coast guys could get there easily and get home at night.

Our range days went up to three a year, capping off each training cycle for all beginners, while the older hands joined in to keep their eye in. Understandably, several other districts used it too, so it was in use most weekends in the year. Apart from the formal target shooting, we learned to get out of vehicles under fire and fight back. Chris would sometimes improve matters by jamming the vehicle door, then explain how to get out by plucking the driver bodily out the side window. It paid to keep a very wary eye on him as he generally had a hand grenade in his pocket ready to throw.

The combat course was fun, with fifteen target plates shot at over, under or around, left or right, while standing lying or squatting at a dozen positions. I declined to go through the tunnel on aesthetic grounds, just saying to the guy posted there: "Consider it done, dear boy." Happily, I could hit ten or twelve plates, while some of the Rambo types with all the extra gear were lucky to hit six.

Chris maintained the gas training by making the trainees run down the slope from the lecture terrace to the river, then up the far slope to a big tree, then back. As they clambered up – pretty much on all fours – he'd fire gas canisters at them or to windward of them, while shouting at them to hurry up. The tree was as far as he could shoot. Mind you, anyone with asthma, a cold, or chest problems was excluded. Though the whole day was good hearty fun, it all had a deadly serious purpose, as in the 1990s the SAP was losing over 200 members a year murdered. By comparison in the whole of the 1922 miners' strike – which was a minor civil war involving regiments of troops and the air force – only a dozen or so police were killed.

Out of interest, field trials of petrol bombs were carried out at our range days. They were thrown at the rock face of the quarry. The best would smash but leave their contents stuck to the rock where they would burn for up to 45 minutes. One way to clean off the quarry face was to fire an RPG at it. We often tried out a variety of handguns and rifles: some, like the old standard .303, slightly antique, others trophies from the border. Being able to distinguish types by the sound of their firing could be useful.

If a petrol bomb lands on the roof of your vehicle you have thirteen seconds before your door and windscreen trims land burning in your lap.

If shooting from behind at a car try to fire through the lights or rear numberplate. These are the softest parts of the bodywork.

At Point, I maintained a list of the reserve members in my unit who were authorised to carry the various arms. In practical terms, if you were not authorised to carry you did not work outside, even if you had passed the written exam. You stayed in the Charge Office. They had to have been on the range with the arm, be able to strip, clean and maintain it, and be reasonably accurate with it. On the last count, some members were absolutely barred. I once, with the range officers, watched in fascination the same elderly reservist mentioned earlier lying prone with an R1 rifle fire off twenty rounds, none of which we could spot. He wasn't on target, he wasn't shooting short, he wasn't hitting the bank behind the target, not even the big hill behind that. On another occasion I saw a new recruit stand flatfooted to fire a shotgun. The recoil knocked him clean over and a range officer caught him in mid-air; otherwise he would have fallen a couple of metres into a drainage ditch and got the firearm dirty. The female members generally fired the shotgun with the butt under their arm as a woman does not have as much muscle across the shoulder as a man, and thus bruises much worse. Although I was as an officer eligible to command a range, I avoided that job whenever possible.

The safe handling of firearms was a constant priority. Every time a firearm was handed over, it had to be made safe. A pistol would have any magazine dropped out and then be double-cocked to ensure that any round in the chamber was ejected. The slide was then held open and the pistol handed over. There were similar drills with other firearms, all designed to avoid accidental discharges. Members were also told not to carry a round in the chamber as a normal thing. When we came to a scene which might be dangerous we cocked our weapons, but uncocked once the excitement was over. I also paraded members on at shift starts, which involved the making safe of their firearms and then their loading. At shift end, they were again made safe when returned to the armoury safe, and the rounds counted back.

The other aspect of firearms handling is the mental discipline. We tried to impress on people that a firearm was basically a tool for killing people. It should therefore not be drawn unless you are prepared to use it; and if you do draw you must be ready to shoot. If you are not, you can be killed for the weapon. To be ready, you must have thought through the implications, and have practised the shooting skills, as in a real incident there is no time to wonder. In addition, if you look efficient and determined you are much less likely to be attacked.

I only authorised myself to carry a pistol and a rifle. At Point, a list was signed off by me and the station commander as a standing instruction to all members. It was kept in the Charge Office in the safe with our firearms. So when a reserve member with ten days' service conned a Charge Office sergeant to give him a pistol and rounds, there was no come-back on me when he went home and blew his head apart. As every vehicle by the 1990s had to have a heavy weapon on board in addition to the members' pistols, the consensus of my unit at Point was that the shotgun was best as not needing precise aiming. Try running a hundred metres and then shooting straight, even when bracing your firearm against a pole, a kerb or something solid. We arranged for two shotguns to be assigned to us and had their butts removed and pistol grips fitted so that each was sixty cms long, which makes it usable inside a vehicle.

Mind you, at close range it is a devastating weapon. A

cash-in-transit van was once ambushed up next the Umgeni river. The two guards in the cab were shot. The third guard, in the back, heard a robber jump on the roof and realised he was going to shoot through the air vent. He fired his shotgun up through the vent hitting the robber as he bent over. When the police arrived, they found his body but his head had been blown into a spray of bone and flesh across the road shoulder.

Contrary to most American cop movies a car doesn't stop a bullet, certainly not a 9mm or anything bigger. Only the engine block and standard cast iron wheels will. Anyone resting his rifle on the roof or hiding behind a door is positively inviting an AK47 round through the car into the stomach. Remember that an AK47 or an R1 round fired side-on can penetrate a railway line.

One fact from the USA that intrigued us, but which happily we never had occasion to test, was that shootouts last on average less than three seconds.

All our official rounds were full-metal-jacket, which is the least damaging. Other rounds we came across were largely forms of dum-dums. The simplest was a soft lead nose. Then came the type with a depressed-saucer-shape nose, with a point rising in the centre for extra spread, and sometimes with a drop of mercury for poisoning under the point. Snakeshot was like a miniature 9mm shotgun round, which could reduce up to two pounds of flesh to mincemeat. Last was the military 7.62mm tumbling round, that had a neat entry wound and an exit wound you could put your fist in.

For a really successful suicide, fill your mouth with water then fire up under your chin. That should take the top of your head, above the hairline, right off.

We were also trained to protect ourselves against hand grenades. At camp training practice grenades would be lobbed at us at random moments. These were hollow with holes in the casing with a detonator inside, which made a nice bang and were strong enough to blow off a finger or two if you were fool enough to hold it. I once surprised and delighted my colleagues when leading the middle rank of our platoon on the march up a dirt road, I made some twenty yards with three strides and a dive into the *middelmannetjie* to avoid a grenade at my heels.

The trick was to dive away from the blast and hide behind the soles of your boots which are best kept firmly together. At worst your feet heal better than your head.

Another time the grenade was thrown across an open-air lecture. Everyone dived, but it had gone to a second instructor who tossed it back. The less trusting of us saw this and moved again. It rolled up to one guy's foot.

"Hey Ames, it's next your boot."

"Ah bullsh–" Bang!

Vast hilarity, though it melted his laces and made the uppers into a tea-strainer.

In my time I often worked inside the Charge Office with new recruits, making them write everything, if necessary to my dictation. This covered all the books, forms, and dockets. Whoever had designed these did a very good job as they had no surplusage, carried all necessary cross references, but allowed space for any combination of circumstances. They had to be simple as nearly everyone using them did so – at least part of the time – in their second or third language. In the quiet times on night shifts or when drafting exams I tried to think of ways to improve them but without success. In my early days, the language used in the books switched at midnight from English to Afrikaans or vice versa, and the radio was mostly in Afrikaans. By the end of the 1980s though, the sheer lack of competent Afrikaans speakers meant that the alternating days fell away and radio traffic was nearly all English.

As training – especially at Point – was continuous, the sergeants and older hands routinely supervised the writing of dockets. We also supervised beat work for those who had passed the written exam, to let them learn how to handle themselves outdoors. Two things they had to get used to: always being watched, and walking straight at problems rather than ducking round the block to avoid them. Then you have to take control of the situation, know what is doable and how to get it done. Important in this was the habit of thinking defensively. To be safe you had to assume that anyone you met might want to kill you, frame you for a crime, or simply embarrass you. That is why we never worked alone, so that there was always corroboration for our words and deeds, as well as someone to cover our back.

I reckoned that a large part of our job, especially when in uniform, consisted of street theatre. The uniform had to be, whenever possible, smart and clean. Your posture had to be correct. Your manner had to be suitable for the situation, something which can only be learned by experience, and is to a large extent determined by the expectations of the audience. For one graphic illustration of this, I can recommend George Orwell's tale from his time in the Burmese police, "On Shooting an Elephant". In simple terms, if you get it badly wrong you can get killed.

Much depended on age, size, colour and background as well as linguistic ability. You have to act a role, be clear, decisive and realistic, not a fantasy hero. It can help to be big or visibly tough. It can be an asset to be older. Body language is vital, especially visible confidence that others will do what you want. (My members told me I used to scare the bad people by talking softly and politely, and smiling, the last thing they expected, and that unnerved them.) One keen little Indian member, who was a waiter, had to be told repeatedly not to approach people like a waiter with a napkin over his arm. He was actually pretty brave, once charging and tackling a large Black man who was trying to fell me with a length of 2x4. The key quality I looked for when considering a member for promotion was the ability to take control and use their initiative safely and effectively.

Taking statements correctly was important. As we often found ourselves taking the first information of crime to open a docket, the complainant or witness was seldom calm. I once had a housebreaking victim tell me her story in *charro* English for 170 seconds talking so fast I could not understand a single word. I found it best to let the story come out once simply so I could work out the basics. I then asked for their names, ID no, addresses, telephones and other contact details. This helped them calm down, get a grip on the facts and give a reasonably ordered and coherent tale. I did once though meet a man with no sense of time or sequence: that was nearly impossible. I read over what I was writing sentence by sentence to make sure they agreed with it. As some people found my handwriting difficult, I often dictated to a junior, who then got the credit for opening the docket – and the possible court appearance.

The pocketbook is a piece of kit that is often overlooked but is vital for a policeman, as is a pen. I insisted on accurate pocketbook entries being made at all times of whom one was with, in addition to times and places, even when nothing happened. That way you could always produce a witness, if, say, you had to give evidence in court several months later. We also noted what uniform or plain-clothes we wore. That way if we ever had to be in an identity parade we could be differently dressed, as we knew that quite often a witness registers clothing rather than a face.

We also always noted which firearms we carried and how many rounds were drawn and returned. These were also logged in registers held in the Charge Office. Officers and NCOs could and did make random spot checks during duties, largely to stop extra or non-standard rounds being carried. Members with their own pistols could carry them provided they were 9mm or .38 and the rounds were full metal jacket. .357 magnums or Colt .45s were definitely not allowed.

The arresting officer always noted details of any arrestee and the paperwork references, partly so he could claim the arrest in our internal records. As a rule about 80% of all arrests were made by some 20% of our members.

We could put anything we liked in them, including sketches of crime scenes, motor collisions, or injuries: in short anything that we wanted to remember in detail, in addition to all the cross-references to the various station records, like the crime, cell, or exhibit registers or the occurrence book, which served as the station diary and was normally written by the Charge Office commander personally, so that he had proper control of that and all other records. Older hands tended to develop a rather terse style, as they found that waffle was pointless and often hard to read. It was also a good idea not to let a complainant bleed onto your pocketbook while you were writing down his details.

Pocketbooks were routinely inspected and signed off by officers and NCOs. I would occasionally put a written instruction in a member's pocketbook, and when it was serious and a disciplinary matter a red ink entry was made. Reservist pocketbooks were kept in the safe in the Charge Office as we only assumed police powers once we had been booked on duty, unlike the regulars who were regarded as being always on duty. Once full they were archived, and a fresh one issued. They held 78 pages, all numbered and bound for security.

An important distinction between us and the military was that we worked in pairs or small groups. Constables therefore had to use their initiative without necessarily referring to their NCOs. In my limited experience of working with the army it seemed that you sometimes needed to go as high as a major to find someone with the discretion we expected from a sergeant.

Radio etiquette had at times to be hammered into some stubborn heads, and others discouraged from making total idiots of themselves. One classic I used as a dreadful warning was the Reservist who came on air to announce he had found a stabbed Black male.

"Is he alive?" asks Radio.

"Let me check ..., er, yes I think so."

"Where are you?" asks Radio.

"Er ... back of the Berea."

At this the mike operator went ballistic. The Berea was over 11km long.

Another which I heard one Saturday from a Berea vehicle was roughly: "We've stopped two white males drinking in a car. We're only Reservists and don't know what to do." This, as you can imagine, was greeted with hoots of laughter by Radio and most other vehicles.

I butted in to say: "This is Reserve Warrant Officer Wade. Where is that vehicle? Stay there till I get there. I will sort this out." This I did. The driver was not drunk but I charged both for drinking in public, gave the two female members a serious rollicking, told them to book their radio and vehicle off and get back in their Charge Office. Dave Fisher then sorted them out. Radio was good enough to thank me for doing this.

Searching was a practical skill we trained the recruits in. Body searches should be done by two members: one searching, the other standing off a few paces with a clear view and his hand on his pistol. The man being searched should be spread-eagled, on his toes with his fingers on the wall and his feet a metre from the wall, so if he tries anything you can kick his foot out and drop him.

I used to conceal four wrapped aspirin tablets and a hacksaw blade on me at the lecture – I would be in a shirt and trousers – and invite a recruit to search me for them, with suggestions from his colleagues. The tablets were normally found if hidden in a shoe or shirt collar, but the hacksaw seldom. That I tucked inside and along my belt.

It is possible to singlehandedly search a number of people,

but they have to lie face-down with their ankles crossed and their hands clasped behind their neck, while lying in a row head to toe. You search the rearmost, then make him crawl to the head of the line. Of necessity, this has to be done at gunpoint. Happily we never had to do this.

On the streets, it helps if the man searching is himself first searched to prove he had no drugs or other items on him that he could have planted on the suspect. Males were not allowed to search females, so in the days before female members were available there were police matrons attached to cell blocks. A practical problem was that girls often carried knives for their boyfriends. Another handy hiding place for a knife is on top of a car tyre inside the wheel arch.

When searching a building it is best to look carefully and use your imagination. Drugs were not uncommonly concealed by dealers in the public parts of a building like the stairwells, to stop us being able to use the deeming provisions of the law to prove possession by a tenant.

Everyone sooner or later had to take fingerprints. The standard form needed both individual prints of each finger, plus the four fingers on each hand as a control. There is a knack to taking good prints, especially as the peculiarities of the loops and whorls tend to be concentrated towards the edges so the roll onto the paper was critical. Tattoos and scars were also noted, though only the CID used the detailed form which divided the body into 47 areas. Jail tattoos were normally pretty obvious as they often had been done using ordinary needles and boot polish or soot, which give slightly uneven lines, while the models for nude woman commonly seemed to be Chinese or Asian. The men we paid serious attention to were those with numbers such as 77, 78, or 28 tattooed on the web between thumb and palm, or on the back of the hand. These indicated membership of a jail gang in a long-term prison like Barberton, for which the entry qualification was a murder, very likely done to order in the jail. If you failed the entrance exam, you became the target for the next candidate.

Another practical skill was the use of the tonfa, that is, the long baton with the side handle. This was a dangerous weapon and needed both skill and discretion to be used properly. Members could only carry one if they had passed a two-day course in its use and had attended annual refreshers. A tonfa can basically be used to swing, to jab and to parry. The side handle allows a two-handed leveraged swing that gives a very fast impact that can break the bones of the upper arm, nose or cheeks among others. Reversed, the short end of the tonfa goes about five cms ahead of your fist holding the side piece if you punch someone. If you hold the tip of the long end, the side piece can serve as a cross between a hook and a lever for a variety of holds on the arms. These can be very effective. I can remember vividly how willingly – no, eagerly – I tried to do a backward midair somersault to avoid my shoulder being dislocated. This was on a course where my partner, to her glee, was the smallest female at Point. I never carried a tonfa as I was already a lieutenant, and did not consider it practical or politic to carry this or a rifle or shotgun. It allows the man in charge not to look too aggressive should photographs be taken, and leaves your hands free, which is useful if you are talking to people. My back-up man though was fully armed.

A slightly less demanding topic was teaching them how to handle court appearances. The key for any police witness is to retain credibility in the face of direct contradiction by the defence. Any show of unease or nervousness tends to make a magistrate wonder, as does a loss of temper. In the early 1970s in Pretoria there was a black, bouncy and rotund defence attorney called Tshabalala who could destroy unenlightened Afrikaner witnesses simply by calling them – after a spell of aggressive cross-examination using the polite form "*u*" for "you" – the familiar "*jy*" instead. There were no jury trials, as these had died out in the 1960s from lack of demand and been abolished. Even then they had been limited, as they were not allowed in cases of interracial crimes, as all jurors were white voters.

I therefore told them to hold the top of the witness box or the microphone rail with their hands to stop them fidgeting, and specifically to check with the tape recorder operator that their voice was being picked up clearly before they gave evidence. A blind prosecutor told me he could hear easily when a witness was lying or just nervous. They should not show any involvement in the case or bias against the accused. Conceding points during one's evidence-in-chief in favour of the accused, such as his co-operation during or after the arrest, even before a defender asked, was a good idea. Also useful was to ask at the end of cross- or re-examination, if you could be excused from the court, as this tended to show a lack of bias. If you did not do this, your subpoena obliged you to stay till the end of the trial and we had jobs to get to. Sitting at the back cheering on or trying to help the other witnesses was unhelpful. I also warned them that identical evidence is most suspicious, as truthful witnesses will always have some variations on the same incident. In addition, the quickest way to spoil the evidence is to embellish or lie, as the next witness will probably contradict you. Members had to be able to admit either that they did not know or could not remember the answer to every question. In simple terms it is far better and more efficient to stick to the truth.

One case I defended was for theft of a crate of cutlery. Two black males took a crate from the back of a van in full view of the storemen who chased them. They dropped the crate and ran off. One was fool enough to wander back past the van again about ten minutes later, was recognised, chased and arrested. After the first witness, he was obviously guilty – but after the third witness neither the magistrate nor I could make any sense of the incident and he was discharged.

We hardly ever appeared in the Supreme Court as only very complex cases went there. Most murders were heard in the Regional Magistrates Courts which could give ten-year sentences, save for drug and weapons cases where they could give twenty-five years. If more was deserved they could convict, and then refer the case to the Supreme Court for sentencing. District courts could give up to three years. Any sentence greater than three months was subject to automatic review by a supreme court judge, who would read the case file, then either confirm it, send it back for retrial, quash it, or where there was a point of law arrange for it to be argued by counsel before him. The judges could call for a review on any case however they heard of it. I knew of at least one case taken up from a newspaper report.

There was a similar system of review for minor offences where an admission of guilt fine could be paid. Provided we were satisfied someone had been correctly identified and had a fixed address, we could issue a J534 form allowing time to pay at a police station or the option of going to court to fight it on a specific day. The fines were set for each magisterial district by the chief magistrate from time to time. Once the fine was paid, the paperwork was scrutinised by a magistrate to check that the offence had been made out correctly and that the fine was correct. If not, you were refunded. If you paid, the offence did not go onto your record, though if you defended and lost, it did. If however we chose not to or could not issue a J534, the arrestee would be held until the next court day, which among other things allowed for fingerprints to be checked for outstanding warrants. One raid on car washers at a supermarket parking lot produced two men wanted for murder.

The exam for beginners covered Charge Office practice. There were a few general knowledge questions which gave 10% to anyone who wasn't asleep. Then they had to write up a crime card, used for simple straight arrests for minor offences such as drinking in public, an accident report for motor collisions; and a docket used for bigger or more complex crimes, together with the various statements and book entries relating to it. Various scenarios were set out so that the recruits had to show some initiative. Sometimes the replies went well wide of the mark, the result of lack of literacy or thought.

Two examples. I sketched a scene where a lovelorn youth went to serenade his true love. As she lived on the tenth floor he took a loudhailer and a friend with a tuba. What, I asked, do you charge the singer for? One answer said to seize the sewing machine. In another, I was looking for a statement to justify a charge of tampering with a motor vehicle. I got: "I observed a W/M approach a car ... he bent over so I arrested him accordingly."

If however I got an answer which was not what I had designed the question for, but which made sense of the facts given, I would mark it on its merits. This though was not common.

As a matter of policy I set the passmark at 60%. This had the effect of making people try harder, and it impressed the regulars, who passed their exams with 40%. Of course you can adjust the difficulty of the paper and/or the marking to achieve any passmark you like. After a bit of tweaking, I got it pretty exactly at a level of competence that meant anyone passing could do a reasonably good job: certainly they shouldn't disgrace themselves.

I also organised a printed certificate, a modest A5 size in blue with an SAP badge, signed and dated, and, when appropriate, showing a distinction. These were handed out at a monthly meeting to applause. I was slightly surprised later to see some of them mounted and in a prominent position on some of the members' lounge walls. It dawned on me that this was probably the first academic success they'd ever had.

One thing we never did was to arrange photographs of

members, either in groups or as individuals, however much they might have seemed a good idea for mementos or for publicity. In simple terms, we did not want to be recognisable in our private lives. Uniform gave one anonymity. One day, in uniform, I stood for some minutes right in front of a woman I had interviewed for half an hour at work the previous day, without her realising who I was. The one exception we made to this rule was the days of the 1994 election which we thought was an historic occasion, but those have never been published till now.

Unless they passed, recruits were not allowed to work outside so it was irritating to have one stall. Such a one was a Black man with a matric who worked as a clerk. He obviously had the brains but had failed twice. So Godfrey and I had a word with him and promised him that if he failed again, we'd jam his head in the grill door on the cell and work him over with tonfas. He decided not to bet that we were joking, and scored 72%. Perhaps the fact that he had a wife and five mistresses had some relevance.

One evening I had a new member with me at the Square's Charge Office. It was pretty quiet so we offered to get an order of cool drinks, burgers and such like from Playfair Road. I took him a short stroll down the road, pointing out the scenery from a policeman's angle. We met a Black male. I told my new man to search him, so he patted him down carefully as he stood with his hands above his head. He turns to me, tells me the guy is clean. I tell him to check his hands. Surprise: tucked under the thumb of his left hand was a matchbox filled with dagga. The outside crew were not wildly thrilled that the appie Charge Office reserve had made the only arrest of the night.

Our female members had to be fairly careful how they projected themselves in a set of fairly male-dominated or misogynist societies. Many men simply would not let a woman boss them, especially in public or in front of their mates. The smaller ones had to realise that in a violent situation they could be picked up bodily and thrown in addition to the normal hazards of stabbing, shooting and such like. They were not allowed to patrol without a male member. On average, interestingly, they were better shots than the men. The female platoon at the police college routinely won the shooting competitions. For a girl, it was much harder to get into the college than into varsity. On the street though, they became expert with their mouths. Some of them were also tough and dangerous street fighters. The small men had the same problem. I remember once tackling a very strong drunk and fighting Black man with five other members. I was able to grab his right arm and handcuff it while the rest, holding his left arm, were all swung in mid-air. We were only just able to get the cuffs around his wrists to the first notch, after tripping him face-down.

Chapter 10

TRAFFIC

Traffic offences were not our primary focus. If we saw something minor like defective lights, we generally ignored it unless we needed a reason to look at the driver. If we thought a vehicle not roadworthy, the City Police (who had a discontinuance book) had to inspect it to have it taken off the road. We did however take action on reckless or negligent driving and drunken driving, most commonly when attending collision scenes, of which there was no great shortage. A scene involving injuries and a drunken driver, or a hit and run, were on a technical basis about the most complex dockets we normally had to file, involving statements, accident reports, plans, medical examinations and blood samples, plus the detention of the suspect and the calling in of paramedics or firemen.

Often the first vehicle at the scene was a tow truck, largely because they commonly had scanner radios that could listen in to the police network. We used them, if the driver agreed, to clear the road and obviously to take them to a repair yard. Drivers quite often wanted an AA service to comply with their insurance. If we needed the vehicle to be examined forensically it was taken initially to the police pound. Before removal, we marked up the position of all the vehicles involved and any relevant debris, bodies or skid marks. I used to carry steel marker crayons for this. These leave bright yellow heavy-duty wax lines on tarmac that can survive a week and more of heavy traffic. A pool of blood vanishes entirely within forty minutes in city traffic. One of the most important items to mark, as it is oddly one of the most easily forgotten, is the direction that vehicles come to rest. That done, we shifted the wrecks, if necessary by hand.

If someone had been injured, we had to draw a plan. Although one could be drawn using triangulation, in real life this was far too complicated and prone to error. We used the line method. In this, you select a straight line running across the scene along a feature that can be found again or accurately reconstructed from engineers' plans if the road layout changes. The obvious one is a kerb or, failing that, a line between two poles (for streetlights, robots or similar), all of which bore reference numbers. You then pick a fixed point at one side from which you measure off distances along the line to the things you want to measure. Next, you measure at right angles to the line to, say, the left front corner of vehicle A, and note the result. As we never had tape measures we would pace out the distances, and to give a reasonably accurate measure of the pace, pace out a measurable distance between say two poles, and on a steep slope pace it both up and down hill. The lengths of skid marks were always measured as accurately as possible so that speed could be calculated. My feet, usefully, were one foot long. The plan and key then went into the docket. Once the Collision Unit got going, we could call them in if there were serious injuries or deaths or a multiple collision (that would probably end up with a third party damages claim). Of course all this only works precisely in a built-up area; in the country you have to improvise with rocks, fences and telephone poles.

Here follow a few of the more memorable cases.

We arrived at the collision scene at the corner of Umgeni and Innes Road. Normally, to check the point of impact you look for lumps of mud on the road. They are knocked out of the wheel arches by the shock of impact, which is very useful when the vehicles have spun away. This time was easier: the whole car floor fell out on the road. It was 90% body putty.

*

We stopped a car one evening on the Esplanade as its rear lights were off. OK, normally we'd leave that to the City Police, but it was a quiet night. As the passenger got out, his door was so rusted that it dropped three inches below the sill and cracked in the middle. To the driver: "Is this car yours?"

"No," says he brightly, "it's a company car."

*

One quality of fibreglass car bodies is seldom advertised. After a crash the fragments of the body panels on the road make a lovely cronch sound, just like when you drive over a rhino beetle.

*

It seemed to us that American cars must be uniquely dangerous as they nearly always burn or explode on or after impact, as proved by the movies. In reality, a car burning is a rarity even if petrol has spilled all over the road. I certainly only once saw a burnt out car. The most spectacular fire was when a petrol tanker caught fire on the overhead section of the southern freeway and set fire to say 200m of the road surface which then melted and started to run onto the lower section.

*

The type of car you pick can make a serious difference to your life expectancy. I've met a man who when driving a BMW 7 series at about 175kph had a head-on into a Mercedes going just as fast: impact speed 350kph. He got out and helped the other driver as his door was jamming. Neither was hurt, except that the bruising from the seatbelts made it hard to breathe for a week.

The Fiat Uno did not give this protection. At 3am one morning on my way home I was second at a crash. First, and ironically also a witness, was a tow truck. The Uno had been going along the right-hand lane of an empty three-lane roadway when it suddenly veered to the right, hit the kerb, bounced up a foot or so, slammed sideways into a light pole, spun around the pole and landed back on its wheels in the right hand lane. The right-hand door column smashed into the back of the driver's head, giving him depressed skull fractures and trapping him. We called in paramedics and back-up. Between about six of us we finally smashed out the windscreen to get him out the car as the passenger compartment was too distorted to open a door. While he was still seated though, he was gurgling, almost drowning in his own blood, and, as he bled, so a line moved slowly down his face. Below his colour was normal; above, the colour of a dirty sheet. The paramedics battled for half an hour but failed.

*

One of the odder crashes took place about thirty metres from Addington's Casualty entrance. A motor bike hit something that stopped it dead. The rider was shot up and forward. His feet caught on his handlebars, spinning him face first into the tarmac, which drove his nose into his brain, killing him. When we arrived, some bystanders were dipping their beads in the blood pool. I'll spare you our comments.

*

A small Toyota 120Y sedan came down the up side of the Northern Freeway one sunny afternoon, head-on into a large Datsun. That had two domes in the windscreen where the driver and passenger's heads had struck. Between the front and back seats of the Toyota lay two women and a baby, all unhurt. Next the car on the verge lay three drunken Indian men literally in a pile, each claiming to be the driver – even arguing about it. We were saved from charging all three for drunk driving when a black out-of-town Reservist eyewitness turned up to point out the real driver.

*

One ironical incident took place when a brewery rep ran down a drunk on the Esplanade. After he was rushed to casualty, we located his building supervisor to get into his flat, looking for his teenage son. We had to take his burning supper off the stove. Later we took his son to see him in intensive care. He was hooked up to an array of drips. From the impact to the back of his head his eyelids had each swollen to the size of half a ping-pong ball.

*

A biker one very wet night aquaplaned into a temporary robot mounted on a one-metre cube of concrete. He knocked this over and was lobbed right over three lanes to land hands-first in the gutter. He had compound fractures of both upper arms. When the nurses cut his jacket off he had muscle tissue dangling from the wounds. It looks like chicken. While he lay in the gutter someone stole his wallet with his month's wages in it, something alas not uncommon.

*

I had one six-month spell when I was a sergeant when, nearly every time I went out, I ended up handling a drunken driving accident, often with injuries, nearly always at the end of a shift. What with marking and measuring the scene, identifying witnesses, making a preliminary test of the drunk driver, organising a blood test at the district surgeon who often had to be called from home by radio control, arresting the drunk, writing the docket and booking in the accused, you'd be lucky to get away within three hours. However, I always thought it worth the effort. My run ended when the fines and jail sentences were drastically raised for a first offence to at least R400 plus one year's suspension of driving licence plus one year's jail suspended for five years, and bail was set at R400, which before the days of ATMs was a real problem to raise after hours.

*

One odd case caught us literally as we were driving quickly back to the Square to book off, and foolishly congratulating ourselves on avoiding all drunk drivers. As we passed a crossroad there were flames some ten metres high from a burning motorbike. A bouncer at the adjacent nightclub found an extinguisher and we managed to put out the flames. It turned out that some defective white teenagers had been trickling petrol from its tank to sniff it. The petrol had trickled down the gutter for some distance until some clown flipped a stompie into it. I then had the pleasure of going into the club and getting the DJ to turn off the music and ask if the owner was there. He was, but it wasn't his happiest moment.

*

I used two tests on the street to check levels of drunkenness. Sometimes a driver is visibly drunk if, say, he has the curried-egg eye, or cannot stand, but these are very inexact. I have seen someone look entirely normal who tested at 0,30.

The first was the nystagmus test which conveniently shows at 0,08 mg of alcohol per 100 ml of blood, which was then the legal limit. Basically, by asking him to watch your finger, you make the driver look as far to the side as possible without moving his head. If his eyes have absorbed enough alcohol the muscles in the eye go into little spasms. This makes the eye twitch. The visible sign is a flutter or twitch of the pupil. The effect on the driver is that the more he drinks the more he develops tunnel vision, which explains why so many collisions take place at crossroads as the drunk simply does not see the other car. In passing, the standard check for drunkenness on a dead driver is to take a sample of the vitreous humour inside the eyeball for analysis.

The second test was not so exact but gave a fair indication. Make the drunk stand upright, feet together and hands by his sides, and tell him to shut his eyes. If he is over 0,20 he'll immediately fall forward. I never saw anybody actually land on his face but it came close at times.

The highest figure I ever arrested for was 0,45 but I heard of a 0,48. Our guess was that above 0,50 would be fatal. For that, depending on body weight, you would have to drink at least three-quarters of a bottle of neat spirits within the preceding two hours or be a three bottles a day man.

We did not use the fingertip to the nose test, or the walking along a line test, as we found that most of us couldn't manage them while sober.

*

One long night, three of us were on uniform foot patrol on the beachfront. We heard the squeal of tyres as a car came too fast down the spiral exit-ramp of a parking garage. As he had to come down Tyzack Street (a single-lane one-way), we stood in the road, halted, tested, and detained him for drunk driving. Later he asked what would have happened if he hadn't stopped but tried to run me down. "I'd have dived on the bonnet," I replied, "and shot you in the head."

"Oh," says he, "they wouldn't do that in Wales."

Later we became quite friendly, especially after he made his phone call. He could only reach his mother-in-law and the whole Charge Office heard and enjoyed her comments.

Then while we were delivering him to Point for detention we saw another car take a corner on two wheels. By now it was 2am and we were two hours past our shift end. My crew and I looked at each other sourly, but our guest pipes up brightly from the back of the car: "He's drunk; you must arrest him." We did, but finished really late.

*

One of the few times I became involved with my partners in our firm of attorneys was in a drunken-driver case. I did not make the arrest, but did a nystagmus test on the woman in the Point Charge Office at the request of my members. It was positive. I told them to charge her. This came back to me as " … then a big brutal cop came in …."

*

One day while strolling back from the office I witnessed a hit and run in Field Street. A Jaguar with a Springs number plate drove into the back of a driving school's car. The driver stopped, paused, then drove off. I scribbled down the details on the margin of my newspaper to make a contemporaneous note, which I would be able to refer to in court, and gave my details to the driving instructor. Later her attorney, after settling the whiplash damages claim on his terms, told me the Jaguar driver had fled as it was her boyfriend's car. He was overseas and she was having a weekend by the sea with another man.

*

Lunchtime one Friday one of my constables John French, off duty, came across a three-ton truck blundering around trying to make a U-turn at the northern end of Point Road. It nearly rammed a taxi. The passenger in the taxi got out, pulled the driver out of the truck, punched him on the nose, got back in the taxi, and left. The driver reeked of booze so my guy flagged down a couple of City Police and asked them to open a docket at Point and he'd put in a witness statement when he got in at six. When he arrived he found to his disgust that they'd put him in only for drunk in public. He was livid, so when I arrived at half past six I discussed the case with him and had a look at the driver who luckily had not yet been released. He clearly had been drinking but it was now over four hours since his arrest. Blood tests had to be made within two hours of arrest to be accepted by a court. He had apparently fallen below the legal limit. After four or five hours the level would drop by more than 0,10 so he could have been 0,18 or more. I decided to go ahead without the blood sample relying purely on French's witness evidence, something rather unusual as prosecutors preferred the certainty of a blood analysis.

At court I was cross examined. "Did my client have blood on his shirt?"

"Yes."

"Was it a lot of blood?"

"About as much as the size of my hand."

"Isn't that a lot?"

"Not at Point."

Even the magistrate laughed.

He was found guilty; but to cap it all it turned out he had no driving license. Then he had a major epileptic fit in the box.

*

I attended court for an early drunk driver case. The defence attorney came to me. "Are you the arresting officer?"

"Yes."

"Aren't you an attorney?"

"Yes."

"Oh shit."

He went off to draft a guilty plea and negotiate a low sentence. I went back to the office.

*

A pompous middle-aged White businessman had been arrested for drunken driving. I came in, busy on another, similar case. He demands: "Why aren't you out doing something useful, arresting criminals?"

"But you are a criminal."

*

Three of us were in a car serving summonses. Helga Slack, one of the first three female reservists in Durban (and who later returned to Bavaria), was in the back seat sorting out the paperwork while I waited at a robot at the bottom of West Street. Suddenly a white car ran fast into the intersection and turned right, passing our right. On his way he hit a pedestrian on a leg spinning him around and over, luckily with no serious injury as he had no weight on that leg. Helga managed to get the registration number as he barrelled towards the beach. I had a half-second view of the driver, my crew half that. We opened a docket for reckless or negligent driving, failing to stop, failing to ascertain injuries and all the rest.

My crew and I went to an identity parade at Point. After some thought, and having the parade turned so I could look at profiles, I picked him out by his facial structure and colouring. Afterwards I remarked that he'd had his long elf locks trimmed off. Yes, was the answer, that was done after the first interview.

Later in court, the prosecutor led off asking my name and rank. He then unusually asked, "What is your occupation?" I looked at him: he had a slightly evil grin. The magistrate noticed the slight tension and looked up. We all looked at the defence attorney.

"Attorney," I replied and watched her breathe, "Oh hell."

She tried hard for three days, but lost.

*

I once found myself on the other side of the drunken driving process. I went to a roof-wetting party at a client's development in Amanzimtoti that started at five. Over the next two hours I had three beers together with a couple of plates of braaied meat and salad. As a rule of thumb the body absorbs alcohol at a rate of a beer an hour, so I would at worst have about one left in a blood count, that is, about 0,025/100mg. The food would slow the absorption, tending to lower the count. The NPA traffic cops were running a roadblock near the river on the way to Kingsburgh. I had some documents to drop off with a client in Kingsburgh so I stopped, and talked to their man, who asked the usual – have you been drinking, what and when have you eaten and drunk. He did the math, looked carefully at me and waved me through. On the way back I got a young keen type who either disbelieved me or was bad at arithmetic. He asked me to park off to take a breathalyser test.

"Oh," says I, "I've never done one of them. How do they actually work?" This he couldn't tell me but started explaining the procedure. "Well, I should register between 0,02 and 0,03 so it'll be interesting to see how accurate it is." He handed me the tube and we fitted it into the machine. I then took a breath which I held in my mouth briefly before blowing into the machine. We both watched attentively. It gave a reading of zero. "It's not very accurate is it? Rather disappointing, I'd say." I strolled off leaving him distinctly fed up.

Two days later I get a call from Sakkie du Plessis, a Warrant in the reserve at Amanzimtoti, and a bloke I'd long known from camps etc. He asked me: "Did you go through a roadblock the night before last down our way?"

"Yes."

"And did you get a zero on the breathalyser?"

"Yes."

"Ah, I thought it was you. We were doing a block last night with the NPA and the one guy was having a moan about this driver who'd been talking, giving him grief about his machine and then telling him it was useless. I got a description of the driver and the car. I told him you were an attorney and a police captain, so he said, why hadn't you said anything? I told him, why should you? But hey man, that was bloody funny. You should've seen his face."

*

In my early days I had to attend a collision on the freeway bridge over the main railway lines at Berea station, all eleven of them. They were powered by overhead lines at 3 000 volts DC which means you fry on them if you land on them. You don't get thrown clear as you would on an AC line. Not a good place to jump even if there are no trains: also an exciting place to chase a suspect, but that I only did once. I was at point, that is, the first policeman to flag down oncoming traffic. A car hurtled down too fast to stop. My problem was which lane to jump from: the left for sane drivers, or the right for the crazies. I guessed crazy.

*

One vexed question for us was when can you or should you open fire on a vehicle in motion. The background to this was that we were facing a variety of groups who for political or criminal ends would happily kill us, so there was a view that we had to get our retaliation in first. On the other hand, unless they opened fire first it was hard to be sure that they deserved it. Unfortunately this was often a situation where a split-second decision by a policeman could be chewed over for weeks in a court. Gut reactions tend to be very hard to explain or defend under cross-examination. The result was that most police, especially the older ones, were reluctant to shoot, save at terrorists or armed robbers. The problem tended to crystallise around car thieves. That said, we assumed any vehicle that tried to avoid a roadblock was carrying weapons or drugs. In my early days I was given an R1 rifle and made point man at a block on the main road to KwaMashu with instructions to open fire on anyone who made a U-turn.

A car that refused to stop when told to pull over took a real risk. As our vehicles never had loudhailers or scroller boards, and seldom had a siren or even blue lights, we generally pulled alongside so our uniforms could be seen, or if in plain-clothes we would show our ID. Happily none of us had any real problems.

*

One night I was on the scene of a crash in Botha Gardens where a car thief had fled after trying to ram a police van. The stolen car was riddled with about thirty rounds, of which only one had hit the driver who had then lost control and gone straight into a tree. The passenger in the back seat was untouched.

Another man was called to say his brand new Mercedes had been recovered after its theft. When he reached the pound he burst into tears. His car had twenty or so bullet holes on the right while the left hand side had wrecked a hundred metres of Armco barrier, and the driver had bled out inside.

In passing, if someone is shot inside a car the odds are that you will have to replace the whole interior trim to make it usable again.

*

One thing we did not do at Point and seldom at the Square was roadblocks. Partly it was the geography, partly the manpower. Firstly, you need a road with no turnoffs to allow evasion, then you need a safe area like the side of a cutting for the riflemen to fire into at the block, and lastly you needed 32 members under an officer. Only the roads along or over the Umgeni River suited.

In the country districts though, like Scottburgh or Amanzimtoti, this was a speciality of the reserve units who seized a lot of firearms and the occasional grenade.

*

A pilot scheme I got involved with at its inception was the Accident Unit, later renamed the Collision Unit, the brainchild of Robbie Askew. He was a Regular sergeant at the Square when he created this and last I heard was the major in charge of all the units countrywide. He hadn't been able to get into the police initially so he did a year as a prison warder. (His most startling anecdote of that period was about the black female chest-to-knee torso used for several weeks by the prisoners as a sex aid.)

He had decided that the handling of serious vehicle crashes by the police was not good enough. This was very much the case in crashes leading to death or serious injury when third party or other claims – sometimes for millions of rand – came up in the civil courts years after the event. The poor cop who'd done his best, perhaps at night in the rain, on a road layout which no longer existed by the time of trial, whose pocket book and notes had been lost, would probably have no recollection at all of any detail.

Again, accidents could simply overwhelm the officers attending. Two examples: first a sugarcane lorry carrying 30 tons loses its brakes on the Berea and demolishes 14 vehicles plus half a dozen pedestrians and two shops; second, a pirate taxi kombi doing 140 kph on the Western Freeway rips off an illegal retread tyre, and does two and a half somersaults down the centre lane throwing most of its 40 passengers across both sides of the freeway where many become roadkill. You definitely need a squad of trained and well-equipped people to be able to record even half the detail.

The other part of their work was to deal with any accidents involving police vehicles, which were self-insured. They could produce and retain detailed draughtsman-standard plans and photographs, and collect forensic data. For example it is possible to tell if a smashed headlight bulb was lit when broken. Robbie compiled checklists for observations to be made at a scene, for which I made a couple of modest suggestions and did the first draft for bicycles. I also gave him a camera and a set of lenses my father had left.

*

Working with him one night we attended a fatal, where a drunk on a 500cc motorbike doing about 80 kph in town hit an elderly Polish veteran, and lobbed his body about 30 metres. Luckily, in a way, he had died instantly, which was shown as his blood merely drained from him. I remember having to decide with Robbie whether the whitish stuff on the tarmac was bone fragments or fish from the takeaway he'd been carrying. I also checked on the bike what was rust and what was human remains. We then capped off the evening by having to inform his next of kin, something always done personally.

While we were examining the scene, the road four lanes wide was largely blocked by police and other emergency vehicles which mounted 37 blue or amber flashing lights. One driver managed to squeeze his way through before we arrested him. He later claimed he hadn't seen any lights.

*

Another strange one at night was when a convoy of three ambulances led by a police car all running fast with lights and sirens went through a six-lane intersection in Old Fort Rd, only for the third ambo to be rammed in the side. It rolled a couple of times while swinging in a quarter circle. Everything in the back, patient, trolley, medicine chest, oxygen cylinders, cupboards and paramedic were tumbled into the road right in front of our foot patrol. We dashed over to help load the patient into the second ambo, which rushed off to Addington. We then helped the crew put all the kit in the back of the ambo before it was towed to a breaker's yard. A little later while we were writing the docket for the arrest of the erring driver, we got a call asking where the man's leg was. Seggie Naidoo went to the yard where he found we had inadvertently chucked the leg which was in a large plastic bag back in the ambo. He came back with it over his shoulder. The patient, who had also had his left forearm cut off in a crash up near Spaghetti Junction, was unsurprisingly dead on arrival.

Chapter 11

THE SPORTING LIFE

One of our routine jobs was the crowd control at sports fixtures, sometimes with regulars, often on our own. The main cricket, rugby and soccer stadiums lay inside the Square's area as did the ice rink, and the bulk of the beachfront, which sometimes was the venue for one-off events such as a street mile or Formula 3 races. The biggest street event was the Comrades' Marathon which for alternate years started their "up" runs next the town hall; on the "down" runs years, when it started at the Pietermaritzburg town hall, it ended at Kingsmead. Point had the rest of the beachfront so it had various surf events but we commonly worked with the Square in their patch as did other units in the district.

*

Kingsmead, the main cricket ground in Natal, fell in the area of the Square. As I knew the ground's administrator, Vic Hohls, and a lot of the local cricket hierarchy and players (after some years as an Intercity league umpire), I often ran the policing of the matches both for the provincial Currie Cup and for limited-over games. Generally a dozen members were enough for a crowd of up to 12 000. Daytime matches were fairly sedate: day/night games were more volatile.

The normal routine was to have four groups positioned at the top of the banks next to the exit stairs, which gave a good view of the crowd and the game. I would be in the main stand with a view of the whole ground – and an excellent line on the wicket. That said, I would from time to time stroll round the ground with my back-up man to check on things, especially the bars behind the stands. The most important circuit though was one before the game started. That I did with my sergeants to pick out the people likely to cause problems.

"Excuse me sir, is this your bottle of cane spirit under your thigh?" might come a friendly voice right in his ear. A sudden glance round would find my smiling face a foot from his.

"Um er erh erm," was a common response.

"Right, I'll give you a choice. Either pour it out, take it back to your car or we can start the paperwork." As the admission-of-guilt fine for introducing liquor into a sportsground was R30,00 (about four times the cost of the bottle or a fresh admission ticket), the emptier bottles got poured but the full ones went out.

This worked well even if there was no liquor, as we'd chat and joke with them. They knew they'd been spotted. For the rest of the day they'd be looking over their shoulders for us and we'd wave to them.

If possible we would bring a truck which was parked off near the nets, if possible sloping down to the rear so it could drain out the back door. Failing that, a van could do. This was used as a temporary cell for drunks, our main problem. As this was summer the temperature inside during the day probably went over 40C. After an hour or two they were shipped back to the Square, but at the end of the day released on a warning, unless they still retained an attitude.

One very useful power I was given by the administration was to be able to close any bar in the ground if I thought it desirable, as most fights or disturbances were fuelled by booze. With experience I could tell when the temperature of the crowd was getting high so I would close the bars half an hour before the fights started. Nothing then happened and everybody went home peacefully.

In the late 1980s a new development was the need to take firearms from the crowd. For this we posted two members in an office in the main stand to receive them, issue receipts and guard them. On a popular night game there could be 200 handguns held.

The actual methods of policing and our conduct were constrained by the presence of TV cameras, as well as the crowd. Some Johannesburg Reservists were fired after appearing on TV sprawled on seats with tunics partly unbuttoned and caps on the back of their heads. If an incident arose at least one camera would be tracking the police reaction. One awkward one was a streaker. Do you give chase all over the ground to the joy of the crowd? No – you go to his friends, seize his clothes and wait for the joke to die a limp death. Ground security could run around. We could not afford to be laughed at. All authority is then lost.

(That lucky exhibitionist had to wait a long time for his chums to remember his existence and make a silver collection.)

The ground had two vocal areas. Castle Corner was where the whites gathered to chirp the players and cheer the girls. If a girl went by to a silence it was a real embarassment for her. Diametrically opposite below the clock was the equivalent Indian area. This had been enforced originally on a racial basis, but even after those barriers fell away the social habits endured.

One day I was showing R/Lt Mac Macdonald around. We were of course in uniform and thus terribly visible. When we reached Castle Corner a couple of wits, or half-wits, greeted us with chirps of pigs, piggy-wiggy, oink-oink and such-like. I looked up at the crowd, spotted the two wide-eyed innocents, greeted them and strolled off, straight to the two hard-looking sergeants from Umbilo who were controlling the bar at the rear. I gave them descriptions and asked them to sort those two out.

They shinned up the bank at the back, then walked quietly down to stand right behind our heroes, who were still celebrating their triumph by entertaining the crowd with repeats. After a bit they noticed the crowd was watching with interest, but not just them. They glanced round to find the sergeants giving them the glacial stare. The crowd enjoyed that. The sergeants stayed there for twenty minutes just to improve their day. Just to rub it in, I greeted them when passing again.

Mind you, the only time I found myself facing a mob was at Kingsmead. The Indian section was unhappy with the Transvaal team and some started throwing bottles and cans at a fielder. This was back in the early 1980s before much attention was given to drinking on the banks. Ten of us deployed along the boundary fence to try to stop the throwing, primarily by telling them not to spoil the cricket. It had nearly died away when some White youths ran onto the field and started throwing the cans and bottles back, not to the boundary fence but into the crowd over our heads. At that a cry went up that "they're throwing at our wives and kids". A hail of bottles, cans, even whisky bottles came down on us and the youths. They threw another salvo into the crowd then left us to be the targets. At this moment the crowd of about 2,000 became a mob. I could feel it as a wild animal presence on the bank, unpredictable and dangerous, quite separate from its individuals. We advanced on them to stop a pitch invasion, driving them back about ten metres. We were too few to split them and were being swallowed up, so we retreated and readvanced a couple of times. We were all splashed from head to foot with drinks from flying cans and bottles. An oldish lieutenant from Durban North, a preacher by profession, was surrounded and drenched. Luckily his nearest colleagues managed to save him before he was felled. Every one of us except me took direct hits from missiles, some being full cans. This was because I kept advancing on the crowd to my front, baton in hand, so the stuff thrown at me went overhead. The players meanwhile had left the field. We then moved off. The mob then reverted to a crowd and slowly simmered down. Later some apologised to me, blaming the white youths. Somewhat to their surprise I agreed with them. Afterwards I was told we'd all appeared on the main TV news.

I had long been amused by the weird cowboy movie cliché: one guy in the saloon punches another and immediately everyone is fighting. But one night at the cricket I saw it happen. I was together with Cst Mullen Deplacido, a martial arts fan from Edinburgh, watching a stand-off between two groups of Indians beneath the back of a stand next a bar. Neither of us was armed. I had a swagger stick, Mullen a tonfa. The two leaders started pushing each other, one swung a fist and all thirty or more were instantly brawling, under a light hail of cans thrown down from the stand. Mullen and I shoved through the fight, each garrotted a leader with a stick across the throat and plucked them apart. The fight stopped so fast that some cans thrown at the brawl landed on the now peaceful group.

One Currie Cup day I was in the stand at the Umgeni end. One vocal chirper was one Bobby from Tongaat who had lots to say about Clive Rice, the Transvaal captain and his team. He and his pals had arrived pretty well oiled and grabbed a good spot on the boundary next the stand. There their comments could entertain the whole stand. This they did at first, but after a while he started to get a bit much. When the crowd started to mutter, I went down to the front of the stand and called Bobby over. His mates watched with amusement, the crowd with interest.

"Hey Bobby, I don't mind you chirping the Vaalies. That's what they're here for." Cheers from Bobby and his mates. "So I'm allowing you one chirp per over but it must be witty; and no repeating." Agreement and laughter from his mates. After that he, and of course his mates, would look up to me in the stand for a thumbs up or thumbs down. This by-play the crowd liked. And we all watched happily ever after.

*

Though we policed a variety of other sports – horse racing, rugby, the Comrades Marathon, boxing, athletics, even motoX racing – these were occasional and generally uneventful. Rugby crowds of up to 40,000 were particularly well behaved, both in the stands and the after-match braais.

Some of the years that we policed the Comrades, we were concerned about the possibility of terror attacks, so on "down" runs we went into the final run-in lap to work out the camera angles on the assumption that any outrage or protest would probably be staged in front of them for maximum coverage. We then watched the crowds from the front in uniform and from behind in plain-clothes. You look for someone who is not watching what the rest of the crowd is watching. This was the era of Bruce Fordyce, who won an amazing nine races in a row. What we actually did most was to help carry runners into the medical tent. They'd finish their 88kms, sit down, chill, turn green, then pass out. The race ended after eleven hours, with the cut off marked by a man on the finish line with his back turned to the runners, stopwatch in one hand, firing a pistol. I once asked the first man in after the gun – he missed by about twenty paces – if he'd try again next year. After a long painful pause, he said yes. The last man in won the Gunga Din Trophy.

*

One fine day at the rugby – a Currie Cup match, a crowd of 40,000 – I was walking around the outside of the stands flying the flag and keeping an eye open for hilarious cooldrink cans falling off the top of the stands. The toilets at ground level were detached brick buildings of a stunning ambience. One of my pet hates was the habit by many of pissing against the outside walls. I came on one such, big, probably a rugby player, dressed in expensively casual gear. As the days of the swagger stick were over I introduced myself by shoving him into the wall by a boot on his arse. He naturally was outraged, but before he could say anything I turned to my colleague, a junior constable, and asked: "How many people do you think could see him here? A hundred perhaps? I think that would definitely rate as exposing in public. Take notes."

I turned to the man, and asked for his name, address, work address, occupation, telephone and fax numbers, all of which were noted. "Unfortunately," says I to him and now also his girlfriend, "there is no admission of guilt for indecent exposure so unless you can get bail you'll be held till Monday when you'll appear in court. But I'll give your firm a ring on Monday morning so they won't be worried by your absence." The firm was a major auditor. By now I had his full attention. "But on the whole I'm prepared to let it go as a formal warning for urinating in public," while looking him squarely in the eye. He took the point, swallowed his pride, thanked me through gritted teeth and left, explaining to his girlfriend what had just not happened.

*

The most hectic job was the all-in wrestling held in the ice rink. The venue held between three and four thousand people, but the exits allowed only five at a time to leave through two double doors and one single. Thick interlocking rubber mats covered the ice as well as the stairs and the raked seating areas. They were old and did not fit too well, making a distinctly awkward footing. We were terrified of any riot or panic, especially as the crowd always included small children, babes in arms and grandmothers in saris. The carrying of teargas was absolutely forbidden.

The crowd was almost wholly Indian so the various Tiger Singhs were the home side and as a rule won. In Cape Town they lost but there the crowd was Coloured and White. The promoters got the crowds going with lots of loud music before and between the bouts. Queen's "We will rock you" or "We are the champions" were the most popular.

Our role was to stop crowd riots, chair throwing and such-like in an arena lit only by the ring lighting. We either sat next the corners of the ring facing out or stood at the back against the walls so that light bulbs, scaffolding clamps or bottles thrown at us from the stands would go over. I once had a one-litre rum bottle fly between my shoulder and ear. I've had plenty of chairs thrown in my general direction when stopping the crowd attacking wrestlers fighting outside the ring.

The fights were scripted, the wrestlers actors, but it was generally good fun, a sort of live cartoon full of kapows, thuds and crunches, with dirty cheating rubbishes being beaten by the good (but not blond) guys. One of the local supporting wrestlers was a Warrant Officer from Chatsworth Police College who used his purse money to put his son through varsity. He one night was repeatedly screaming in the ring while The Spider gouged his eyes. When soon afterwards I asked how his eyes felt, he didn't at first know what I was talking about.

One of the funnier nights featured Tiger Jeet Singh versus Mike Schutte. Mike was an ex-boxer a heavyweight, a well-known character nationwide, called by many comedians *Ou Maaik*. He had an amiable round face, no neck, a blond fuzz everywhere but the top of his head, long powerful arms, big hands and a massive oval body. If backlit by the floods he looked like a killer peach. He later contrived to put out a video of him playing his guitar, seated on a hay bale in a farmyard with lambs at his feet, while he sang a sentimental ballad.

Meanwhile back at the rink. Round one: Tiger jumps into position for the first grapple. Mike looks, thinks, remembers the plot. Mike wins the fall. Howls of abuse from the crowd. Round two: Tiger leaps into position, Mike again looks, thinks, remembers. Tiger wins the fall. Cheers all round. Round three: Tiger gets into position, Mike looks, thinks, forgets. He punches Tiger in the face, knocks him out for several minutes, is promptly disqualified. Pandemonium, even the loudspeakers couldn't be heard, Tiger leaves on a stretcher, we escort Mike out under a hail of cans, bottles, chairs, anything not bolted down.

Quite often wrestlers would throw each other out of the ring to carry on fighting next the officials, us and the crowd, who got really excited. I like most of my members had at times to stop the crowd hitting the wrestlers over the head with a chair while they in turn hit each other with chairs. Scalp wounds spray blood and that really gets things going. One blond American called Beautiful Bobby specialised in gory head butts but sometimes got carried away ... bodily, from under the ring.

Another memorable night which I didn't see, as Denise McCormack (then a Warrant) was in charge, ended in uproar with a local politician called Rajbansi giving a rousing – if not inflammatory – speech from the ring. I gave instructions that if it happened again someone should go under the ring and unplug the sound system, something my Indian members were looking keenly forward to do. Rajbansi, a Chatsworth butcher, had managed to make his way to the leadership of a pro-government Indian political party in the Indian "parliament". He was widely reckoned to be a sell-out and personally ridiculous by his fellow Indians.

*

Greyville Racecourse, the home of the Durban July Handicap, lay in Berea's area but we with other stations helped out on July day. One time I was in uniform with Harry Taylor, one of the Berea sergeants, at the gate between the Gold Ring and the

Owners' Enclosure. We were most amused to be high-hatted by all the Hooray Henrys and Henriettas passing by. He was the director of a substantial local subsidiary of a big British multinational, and they might even have needed one day to ask us for a job.

*

We were asked once to police a motoX meeting. It turned out the licence holder wanted us to stop others bringing beers into the stadium, which was the law so we did that. But we also told him that his beer had to be drunk inside his licensed area, a pub at the top of a stand, so we blockaded him, to the amusement of the meeting's organiser, who had not asked for us. I also took the trouble to check all the conditions and plans of the liquor licence. I reported that we were being used for financial gain. They never asked us back.

*

A disastrous venue was the main tennis stadium. I once went there, asked by the Mayville Reservists to see if I would be interested in deploying some of my people to the cage wrestling events there. The layout of the courts and stands allowed attacks from above by the crowd on wrestlers between the change rooms and the cage. The main entrance from the street was on a downslope with a mesh fence which could be and was pushed down by the press of people trying to get through an inadequate set of turnstiles. Then, around the cage which was on the main court, all the seating was loose metal frame chairs, several of which were thrown at me. Luckily I had borrowed a tonfa so I could catch most with that. The crowd was rather out of control. The reason for this, and the crowning touch of the day, was the promotor's security guards. These were from The Ark – a refuge for the homeless, often former or would-be former alcoholics or junkies, or people with various mental weaknesses. This squad could just about march against a stiff breeze. I reported that the place was seriously unsafe, and that the promotor had no serious intention of securing the venue. Further police cover was refused.

*

For some years a Tattoo was held in Durban. This was designed in part to showcase and encourage the services, who were then fighting a border war. The first – held in the Kings Park rugby stadium – was pretty dramatic, with troops landing from helicopters for a mock fire fight. Later they tended to be more band orientated, with the Prison Service band memorably parading in the dark with lights in their caps flashing in time to the music.

One consistent item was the naval field gun race with two teams racing to dismantle their gun, carry it over a wall and a "ravine", reassemble and fire it. At the end the team had to secure their gun and close up, at which point the petty officer in charge would fire a blank from his pistol to signal his team's finish. This year they were in an arena and we plus some regulars were policing the crowd. Suddenly a message comes to us that someone in a box has been shot. This surprised us. When we reached the box, we found half a dozen men drinking cans of lager. We thought, as the incident happened immediately after the cannon fire, he had been struck by a fragment of wadding from a gun. He protested that it was a bullet that had gone through his upper left arm between his ribs and the arm bone about ten cm from his heart. Luckily he suffered no serious damage. Only when we saw the hole punched through the metal air conditioning trunking behind him did we really believe him. Bertolotti managed to open the trunking and wriggle down to get the bullet, which looked like a stubbed-out butt. One of his mates had felt the wind of the bullet across his nose.

As the only firearms in the arena belonged to the two petty officers I got hold of the lieutenant in charge, to find that one had not been carrying his service Star pistol loaded with blanks but his identical private arm with live rounds. The lieutenant reckoned he might as well resign the next day when he got back to Simonstown, as he was responsible for not double checking the pistol even though they had done this many times and just come back from a visit to Taiwan. What baffled us all was that the shot had been fired into the ground, which was bark on sand to accommodate the horses, but must have ricocheted into the box. On the instruction of a regular I opened a docket for attempted murder. The only good news was that it hadn't hit the guest of honour, two boxes to the right.

*

I only ever policed one soccer match, the first international by South Africa, against Cameroon at the Kingsmead soccer stadium. That had one big concrete covered stand with the rest open banking. On the night a thunderstorm broke over the ground so everyone from the cheap seats ran into the main stand. They then started singing the SA team song Shoshaloza, which for reasons I have never understood is about catching a railway train to Rhodesia, and with heavy stamping on the shoshalozas. The impact made the whole ten-storey stand jump and boom, and for us standing nearby under cover, the ground under our feet also hopped. We won by a single goal.

*

Baboo Ebrahim was a spin bowler who played for Natal. I was standing in a club match when he bowled a ball that bounced about four inches high and shot towards the wicket. The batsman, like the rest of the field a White guy, jammed a bat down onto it, looked up and asked "What the hell was that?" "Oh" replies Baboo, "that's my speciality: a coolie-creeper". Two seconds of dead silence: then we all fell about.

Chapter 12

POLICE COLLEGE

In my day there were four police colleges. The largest was that for Whites in Pretoria West, the Black one was fifty or sixty kilometres north of that at Hammanskraal, the Coloured one at Bishop Lavis on the Cape Flats, while the Indian one was in Chatsworth near Durban. All recruits went to one. Until about 1980 entry could be with a Standard 8 certificate to do a police matric in a one-year course, or with a matric for a six-month course. After that, entry was only with a matric, partly to produce more recruits, partly as Standard 8 disappeared as an acceptable school-leaving qualification. Courses were given for detectives, forensics and other specialist fields such as vehicle theft, and officer entry, lasting from a few weeks to three months. A separate staff college was created for senior officer entry at Graaff-Reinet and later at Wellington. There was no separate officer entry: everyone had to come up through the ranks. It was possible if you were a graduate to get accelerated promotion to Warrant Officer in a specialist department such as forensics after a one-year course. Graduates were very rare, save for a few ambitious officers who did B Pol – a degree I thought somewhat misdirected as it was full of criminology and sociology but wholly lacking in man management or logistics.

With a bit of luck a Reserve member in line for promotion to lieutenant would be sent to the college for the reserve officers' course. The regulars did a thirteen-week course of which three weeks were dedicated to riot platoon drills. We covered the same ground in two weeks without riot work (bar a lecture on the theory and practice), as we were not expected ever to have to handle riots. This simply was because we did not have the trained manpower or the time. Riot platoons were often on fulltime standby in the most remote or isolated places for days or even months, most of which would be spent watching and discouraging faction fights or other violence. The classic unit was the old mobile unit in the Transkei – some 400 strong – used to stop interclan wars with several hundred a side. By the 1980s the units based in the major cities had Casspirs; these were armoured vehicles that carried a driver, a gunner for the twin 0,5 machine guns, and twelve men in the back. These had been developed for the fighting in South West Africa where they were used by Koevoet, the SAP's counter-insurgency unit, with much success. The crew could fire live rounds and gas or hand grenades through ports, upwards and to the sides, the rear, and importantly, underneath the vehicle. They could survive land mines and RPGs, and still drive away. They could also usefully machine-gun the base of the wall of a house, then knock it over and drive over the debris to deal with any occupants. Later came the smaller Nyala, a sort of armoured bus/truck, but that could be disabled by a hand grenade thrown underneath to sever the hydraulic controls. Each platoon was armed with gas and smoke canisters, rubber rounds, plus the usual range of weaponry. Each also had a photographer to film any action, and a scribe to write a running timed account of all events especially all commands given. The commander was also recorded on tape, both on the spot and where possible at the local radio control. But I digress ...

I flew up to Pretoria for the course. The course leader came down on the Sunday afternoon to the terminal to collect me, which I thought friendly. He was a Major Stumpke, a huge guy at least 6'4" tall but wide with huge hands. He described himself ruefully as a *rugbywrak*, but there was no way I would ever think of trying him on. He was a really nice guy.

The speed of our course made us rather special in the eyes of our lecturing staff. They found us intriguing, partly because we were prepared to do their job working without pay in the sewers of society, but mostly because of our varied experience, abilities and professional skills. On my course, out of the eighteen of us we could have set up a property development syndicate, as there were builders, electrical contractors, builders' merchants, a quarry owner, a quantity surveyor, an insurance broker, an accountant, an attorney, a bank manager even a *dominee* to open *met gebed* [with a prayer]. All we lacked was an architect and that we thought no lack. Other guys included a teacher, a loss adjuster, a dairy farmer and a senior civil service type, assistant secretary or some such. Apart from the more obvious spots such as Jo'burg and Pretoria, we came from centres like Queenstown, Kuruman, Vryburg, Secunda, Margate, Klerksdorp and Potchefstroom.

As a footnote I had discussed with some of the staff their pending move to Wellington, and their worries about housing down there. They were astonished when I phoned them a week after the course to give them details of good but affordable areas or suburbs, agents and even a builder who would happily build them their own little estate.

The man from Kuruman was the biggest though not the tallest in the class. He had originally gone there to play rugby for Stellaland, and he must have been a truly frightening opponent. His idea of really finishing off a grudge fight was to knock his man unconscious by throwing him into a wall and then pissing on him. No one disputed that.

The dairy farmer, my room-mate, was another rugby type. He played prop for Queenstown and though he was three inches shorter than me was so barrel-like that I couldn't get an arm far enough around him to be able to bind on him when some of us were playing *foefie*-rugby in the corridor. He was the guy with the shortest service period – a little under nine and a half years, about four months less than me. The longest-serving man had done seventeen years.

The quantity surveyor had been a regular Warrant Officer in the presidential guard unit. They mounted the innermost guard on the state president and prime minister, in the capitals and also at their holiday homes. There things were pretty informal. He spoke well of Tini Vorster as well as her husband John. At Oudebos he would drink coffee and chat with them on occasion, while Tini also every night checked that the night shift had thermoses of hot coffee, sandwiches, fresh vetkoek and such like to keep them going. Mrs Donges on the other hand rated them one notch above the binmen but didn't give them any Christmas box.

The dominee was a Hervormde Kerk man from Secunda, but lived before that in Rustenburg, which had helped him become a *fynproewer van mampoer* [connoisseur of peach brandy]. As the Hervormde was the most conservative of the three Dutch Reformed Churches the class anticipated a few sparks between him and me, as I quickly proved to be the most voluble of the five or six *Engelsmanne* [Englishmen] in the class. Coincidentally he sat at the right rear, I at the left front. Certainly we gave more than our share of answers and questions in class and often did differ, but politely or humorously. Word spread among the lecturers who often walked in and started: "*Wie's die prokureur*? And for what I am about to say, *'skuus dominee.*" [Who's the attorney? ... and pardon me, minister.] In fact we got on well both personally and intellectually. I remember one night walking long and slow along the perimeter fence looking for sticks to make into play-play swagger sticks for drill while discussing sin and redemption, and handing steakburgers to the perimeter guards.

As an aside, a friend of a friend of mine was in a res [hall of residence] at Tukkies (that is, the University of Pretoria), when Vorster was prime minister. He was the jester of the *huiskom*, the residence committee, and among other things had worked up a very lifelike imitation of the PM. One day Vorster who was chancellor of the university arrived with his wife for lunch with the *huiskom*. All went splendidly albeit doubtless *bedeesd en bedaard* until Tini turns to him with a winning smile and says, "I believe you do a very good imitation of my husband. Please do show us." And he had to. Tini laughed heartily, as did the *huiskom*. John watched drily and remarked, "Very good, but don't give up your day job"

Our status in the college was quite distinct. We alone wore field dress with white epaulette flashes, which meant that most recruits had no idea who or what we were. As a result they generally saluted us even at the double, to which we responded affably and with dignity. They had to go everywhere outdoors at the double; we did not. We were all about forty to fifty years old, all pretty well off, driving Mercedes, Audis or similar – in other words possessed of fuck-off money, and used to running things. Mind you, we did have one Fotherington-Thomas type. We were merely surprised he had not been murdered.

A drill sergeant – normally the terror of the recruits – gave us drill, specifically the motions for the swaggerstick. He didn't know whether to laugh or cry, but after each session late in the afternoon, we took him down to the NCOs' mess and bought him a few rounds. He decided to laugh.

Meals – brunch at nine and supper at six – were in a big mess hall where our tiny group of eighteen occupied a pair of tables. After a couple of days, the other course groups around us began wondering why we had immediate and constant attention from the waiters, second helpings, extra steaks and all. Easy: we bet the waiters R10 per table they couldn't find us seconds. Before we left they were trying to win R20 by bringing crayfish.

Our other "meals" were coffee/tea and rusks at about 0600, 1330 and 2000. The quality was not great, but at least the morning one was hot which helped us get our brains going for the first lecture. The most surprising thing I saw on the second Monday morning though was the hills across the valley. The smog had been so bad through the first week that I'd never seen them.

The evening one was as a rule ameliorated by a few bottles and some discussions both interesting and very wide-ranging. One night we started analysing each other. Given our experience the observations were distinctly sharp, and blunt. The consensus on me delivered by the quantity surveyor, was that though I was low-key and polite I would be a bad bastard to cross.

On the middle Sunday we held a braai for the teaching staff, the top brass of the college and ourselves. Largely as I was going to be in Pretoria over the weekend staying with friends, I was given the job of organising it, though grave doubts were expressed as to what they could expect from a *soutie*. I asked my hosts for the best German butcher in town, went there and got well-hung steak, and four types of sausage. I prepared salads and a dressing, got lots of rolls and spent the change on pudding – a bottle of malt whisky. It went well. We ended up handing out left-over steaks to the perimeter sentries. I nearly got the nickname of "Proppie" [Corky] for handing out the whisky by the capful to the needy.

Classes tended to be lively, particularly when we got into personal anecdotes. Between us we had a very wide range of experience both urban and rural, across different languages and societies, and wildly varying ranges of crimes. For instance the only livestock case I had ever met was two men trying to slaughter a goat with a dinner knife in a parking garage at 1 am. The country boys were startled by the number and type of places drugs could be hidden and the vagaries of our whores.

The one lecture that silenced us all was a movie session. The first part, taken from a foreign news crew, was of the murder of an old black woman in a township. She was alleged to be an *impimpi*, a police informer. She was stoned, finally with lumps of concrete a metre long, then set on fire, while every so often youths would run and jump over her to kick her in the head. This did not silence us, though it did tend to reinforce our opinions of the opposition.

The second part was an SAP video taken at a murder scene near Jo'burg. A Black man broke into a suburban house. He raped and strangled the housewife, then hanged her body by the neck from a rafter in the garage using clothes line. As each of her three children, aged eight to fourteen, arrived home from their schools, they too were strangled and hung in the garage. Last came the husband. After a serious struggle he too ended up in the garage. When the police cameraman arrived, the bodies were still swinging and twisting slightly. The killer was tracked down from the pressure imprint of a telephone number he jotted down on a pad. When the film ended there was two minutes of total silence.

Our lectures otherwise covered, among other things, practical leadership, administration, handling of scenes of crime, the theory of weapons handling and use, and the control of ranges. I found interesting the three types of leadership: the consensual, which works well if there's time for discussion as in monthly meetings; the laissez-faire, where basically you tell your juniors to sort it out; and the do this/follow me approach, which is vital in fast moving or dangerous situations. I found it worked well in practice under normal circumstances to let my sergeants and more experienced members take the initiative but to watch quietly over their shoulders and make the occasional suggestion. I seldom had to intervene other than respond to a question. The fact that I walked beat with them rather than ride in the car or van stopped a lot of disputes about who went in the vehicle, and allowed me to know more precisely what was going on. By doing this a better mutual understanding and efficiency could be built up. When the bullets start to fly however, it is vital that one competent man, or woman, is clearly in charge so that decisions can be taken and acted on fast.

The theory was useful in that it gave structure to things we had had to deal with perhaps in fragmentary fashion using what we hoped was common sense. The course was designed to allow us to understudy our station commanders.

At the end we sat an examination which we all passed. The class average was 89% which really cheered our course leaders. They told us that when our class was commissioned there would be 268 officers in the reserve countrywide.

Our biggest wow moment though took place on day one when we were taken to Aladdin's cave, the Quartermaster's Store, and kitted out. We saw stuff we didn't know existed. We got kit that fitted, piles of it: stuff we normally waited months to get if at all.

Chapter 13

CHILDREARING

Our members who had children, especially those who were single parents, had of necessity to think through how their kids would deal with their police activities. As a rule they would be brought along to the social events, so they would meet your colleagues and be known to them, but for the rest they were kept well clear of our active service.

I once took the children on a VIP tour of the police forensic laboratory in Pretoria – a friend of a friend ran it. They were both young, about ten and twelve. Drew thought it all sort of cool and fun till the lab technician handed him two items that solved a shooting case: two skull pieces with bullet entry and exit holes in them. He stayed interested. So too did Fiona.

Occasionally while off duty I used to give them a policeman's tour of central Durban. I showed them scenes of murders and other crimes, places where market women slept, where vagrants and homeless people camped. Black women, say 200 of them, used to huddle up inside the main gateway to the English market. Vagrants got under shop canopies or other overhangs, or under trees or bushes in the parks to avoid the rain, used wooden pallets as mattresses, and plastic sheeting or similar as blankets. Fortunately no one ever died of exposure. Drug dealers spread pretty wide but certain areas had higher concentrations, such as Point Road's northern end, and the vicinity if not the interior of night clubs. I also showed them, from a distance, some of the street whores, and some of the massage parlours.

This gave them a graphic picture of the bottom of the human pyramid: very motivational.

Fiona used to get rather frustrated in her mid-teens about clubs. A fair number of her classmates used to go clubbing though still underage, relying on the clubs being taken in by makeup, poise, and fake or borrowed ID books. We in the police would randomly visit the many drinking spots looking for underage kids, whose presence represented a breach of the clubs' liquor licences. That could lead to fines, or if they were persistent, the loss of the licence and the banning of the licencee. Because Fiona had been around too many police functions, nearly every Reservist from Point to Tongaat knew her by sight, and of course whose child she was. (We once arrested a police colonel's wife and two daughters in a nightclub.) She couldn't go anywhere.

Fiona and Drew got to know Point and its people rather well from the occasional visits to the station or the various outings or functions. Point had braais, some at Shongweni Dam and later, when John Baldock acquired a speedboat, up at Hazelmere Dam where waterskiing was allowed. Generally our people split into two groups, the younger lot who drank cane and listened to heavy metal and such like, and the somewhat older who preferred silence and whisky. The energetic, which included Drew, would dash off to the water and try their luck on skis.

One Saturday I was helping to give a training seminar but had to pick up Drew from Cordwalles, his school in Pietermaritzburg. I turned up an hour late in full uniform, medal ribbon, sidearm and all, which surprised the other pupils, all perched waiting on a wall.

"Why are you late?" asked a rather peeved Drew.

"I had to deal with a fatal on the way up."

"Oh, how many killed?"

"Only one."

This drew a rather wide-eyed response from his classmates.

On the way back I pointed out the scene, north of Camperdown. The car was still standing on its nose on the median propped up by a large bush. When I'd arrived the driver had been trying to climb out the rear windscreen, bellowing with fear and frustration. His wife of two weeks, a pretty girl, lay on the grass quite some distance ahead. Her right hand bar some skin was severed. Her head had been crushed at the rear. A piece of kikuyu grass was lying on her open left eye. She was not bleeding. She was clearly dead. They were returning from their honeymoon when they came off the road.

Drew got a first-hand introduction to death. One evening we were going home from my office down Innes Road when we came on a crash scene. An elderly couple on their way to a dinner party had made a U-turn into a parking spot next their friends' house. She didn't see a motor bike following which went straight into the side of her car. The biker, middle-aged, slammed forward into the handlebars and column. He was not happy. He was not bleeding from the mouth, but we were worried he might have internal injuries. A stomach rupture could kill him in five hours. We were persuading him to at least see his GP, and the old man, the passenger in the car, was chatting to his hosts at the roadside. He started towards us, then fell sideways onto his back. I ran over to check on him. As I got down face to face the light in his eyes faded out. It took two to three seconds. The muscles in the face relax which allows the cheeks and eyes to fall in a little. A doctor and a nurse lived nearby and came at once to do CPR, etc. I went to get drugs at the nearest emergency chemist. Drew got the job of holding a saline bag above the body. Everyone carried on for half an hour but he died. I've often thought that as a last view, my face close up must have been pretty dire.

Childrearing

Fiona once remarked that I wasn't like other fathers. When I enquired why, she replied that they came home and read the paper: I came home, then went out hunting. The children also told me that they could easily tell when it was time to stop doing something. I changed to my police face.

We used to go every year to the Royal Agricultural Show in Maritzburg. They liked the ice creams and balloons, the book stall and the steaks, and the various arena items. I went more for the livestock. One year however the SAP put on an exhibit of drugs showing how they looked, how they were prepared for sale and some photos of addicts. The most graphic was a series of a girl from age 16 when she was first arrested for dagga, to 28, when she was a heroin addict on a mortuary slab. I was strolling around with the children, then about twelve, discussing the various exhibits, their prices, their availability, their dangers and effects. The local narcotics policeman on the stand started taking an interest, probably when I was telling them how to check dagga for pawpaw leaves. They used to be chopped up, dried, and used to bulk up the dagga. He became more and more curious till I explained who and what I was. Then it was handshakes and jokes all round.

They both came closest to a real-life incident one New Year's Eve down at Stellenbosch. As we walked down the lane next to what was then a drinking establishment at the Coetzenberg Hotel, generally known as Tollies, two Coloured men dashed out, the one chasing the other and beating him over the head with a bunch of flowers. They soon came back and went inside. We were window shopping when they suddenly reappeared, this time with the flower wielder being chased, but with a long knife. I scooped the children up and jumped into a shop. The assistants locked the door. I then went out to assist any police. The pair had been stopped next the post office without very much blood spilled. I told the policeman I would let them have a statement at the nearby station. I went down with the children to the Charge Office expecting an attempted murder charge but they had simply given a warning for disturbance. The Charge Office sergeant just reckoned: "Ja well, it is New Year's Eve".

Chapter 14

THE 1994 ELECTION

The 1994 election was for us an interesting time. No one really knew what to expect. Nearly a million extra citizens came out of the hills and townships to get ID so they could vote. No one was really sure what facilities would be needed for voting. The election was extended from one to three days simply to allow the huge queues of the first day to get through the polls.

The security situation was also volatile and uncertain. Party activists around the country were being murdered. In KwaZulu-Natal there was a low level civil war in progress between the ANC and Inkatha which had led to perhaps a thousand deaths in the previous six months or so. Rumours, which we thought unwise to disregard, were rife of weapons caches, enough for an eighteen-month campaign, held by those two parties plus some far-right-wing but undefined White groups.

As background you have to remember the following unofficial history, much of which I heard anecdotally but which I believe to be broadly accurate.

When Natal was formed in the nineteenth century, the local blacks were either Zulu in the broad sense, or not. The Zulu clan which produced Shaka was small, never more than a few thousand. The Zulu state created in the first quarter of the nineteenth century by Shaka, largely by conquest, consisted of a number of clans of which the largest was the Buthelezi, which in my time had over 300 000 members. The chief of that clan could therefore call out the biggest clan army. As a result, the chief of the Buthelezis was for over a hundred years the hereditary prime minister to the Zulu king. In 1994 Chief Mangosuthu "Gatsha" Buthelezi had been in place since the 1960s. In the 1970s and 1980s he had created and developed Inkhatha, initially as a traditionalist cultural organisation, but increasingly as an overt political party of a conservative type that was within limits prepared to co-operate with the National Party government, who naturally were happy to use it as a counter to the ANC and PAC. The non-Zulus in Natal, who had been refugees from the Shaka wars and the ghastly ripple effects of the Mfecane, lived in the western and northern areas of Natal in reserves created in the 1850s by Sir Theophilus Shepstone, whose Zulu name was Somtseu. The biggest group was in the Edendale area, west of Maritzburg. They formed regiments, even one of mounted infantry (the Edendale Horse), to support the settlers in the war of 1879 against the Zulu under Cetshwayo, and in 1899 against the Boers. They tended to be better educated and more urbanised than the Zululanders. In my day they were largely impervious to the attractions of Inkhatha and supported the ANC.

The geography of Natal allows basically a coastal route from Durban north-east and south-west and a westerly route to the Drakensberg, then either north to the Transvaal or further west to the Free State. The Transvaal route carried the vast bulk of business, and the biggest towns and coal mines lie along it, thanks to the railway which started in a humble fashion in 1860 connecting Durban to the harbour at Point, but which reached Johannesburg in the 1890s. Railways were similarly built up and down the coast. Till then goods went to Port Shepstone by sea in large part, as there is a river every five miles or less.

In the 1980s the ANC–SACP alliance sent a squad of its armed cadres into the Durban Pinetown area to challenge the

Inkhatha who then held sway. This was part of the armed struggle then enthusiastically supported by the SA Communist Party, which in turn was encouraged by the Russians. The ANC started as a political movement in 1912 and had only taken up the armed struggle in about 1961, when it formed Umkhonto weSizwe ("The Spear of the Nation"), under the command of Nelson Mandela, who seems then to have been a member also of the SACP, which gave the ANC a component also devoted to a military takeover. This for them was never a wholly exclusive approach though it was often so depicted as part of the so-called "total onslaught" of the 1980s. The two strands were seen by nearly all Whites and most of the Indian and Coloured communities as terrorists, and as such disliked and resisted. These were opposed by the right wing in the NP government, then under P W Botha, and the parties to its right, and the armed forces who thought a military solution possible. The collapse of the USSR in 1989 killed off any hope of Russian support, which had already been diminishing. Oddly, the ANC and SACP had been told as early as 1978 that the campaign should be basically political with the military aspect only an adjunct, and that by General Giap, the Vietnamese commander who defeated both France and the USA. That insight however had not reached the lower ranks, who still believed a military takeover was possible. One real concern in the 1980s was the possibility of a rerun of the wars in Angola, Mozambique and Rhodesia, or yet worse, the Algerian civil war of the 1950s. In the years leading up to 1994 there were a lot of political negotiations between the ANC and the NP, after 1989 under De Klerk, but these were then wholly unknown to us. With the benefit of hindsight, the truly remarkable political achievement of Mandela and De Klerk was to rein in their military enthusiasts on both sides, and to allow a peaceful transition rather than a civil war. At the time we reckoned we were close to the edge and that any major incident could set off, at the very least, wide-spread rioting which the police and military would find extremely difficult to control. In Durban for example, there were less than 5000 police to control some 3 000 000 people spread over say 2000 sq km; in other words, with the usual four shifts, each policeman would have to control over 2400 people.

The ANC squad did fairly well, moving into protection rackets, armed robbery, drugs and vice to support themselves in the manner to they wished to become accustomed. Weapons came from Transkei, then an ANC stronghold, even from Gen Bantu Holomisa's army's armouries which SA supplied. The ANC then told this group to go north to Maritzburg, Howick, Estcourt, Ladysmith and Newcastle to repeat the process, while a fresh group of cadres would take over on the coast. The first group were well settled and refused. The ANC cut off their weapons supply and sent another group to kick them out. Bear in mind most of the ANC's best organisers were also members of the Communist Party.

To replace their weapons supplies the first group then joined Inkhatha which got theirs largely from Mozambique, where conditions in the 1980s after their civil war were so dire that a sack of mealie meal could get you an AK47 and 200 or more rounds. From about 1985 there were a series of political and/or criminal assassinations throughout the province. ANC support and the small amount of PAC supporters were found in certain parts of the bigger towns and the cities plus Edendale. The rest, especially the rural areas, was pretty much Inkhatha. If you were not in the right area you could stay provided you shut up. Putting up a poster could be ill-advised. Demonstrating very likely would be. The locals might give you a hint of this by burning down your house. In extreme cases they first ran wire around the house across your windows and doors, and killed you with axes or spears or firearms if you tried to get out.

To return to 1994: the police and army were mobilised to deal with whatever might happen. For the first time in my police career the reserve force was called up for continuous service, which meant we were paid. At Point, 22 of us paraded on in full uniform at 0600 on the first election day, armed up, and went to monitor polling stations in our district. As the day progressed Durban proved to be peaceful. All my people voted, though we did jump the queues which were three hours long at Addington School.

Reports came in of localised rioting and crowd problems. Together with other Reservists from District 46 we reported to the Square. We then worked out who could be sent out of town and who must stay – basically those with family or unavoidable work commitments. Ten of us from Point could go. We went home and got some kit. I got anti-malaria pills for us all. At first there was the suggestion that we would go to Vryheid by helicopter, which would have been interesting, but finally we were detailed to go to Sundumbili, the black township next to Mandini in Zululand, in a weary old police bus.

We arrived at the KwaZulu Police station there well after dusk, to the surprise of their night shift who knew nothing of us. There were a few others with us including a stray Reservist and a black Lieutenant Manzi from the Computer Unit, both from the Square. After some discussion the troops were given a recreation room as a dormitory, while I got the station clerk's office as officer's quarters. We all slept on the floor but I could double up a carpet. The station clerk, an oldish Zulu Warrant Officer, was most surprised and not best pleased to find a White officer pulling on his boots when he arrived in the morning. We were lucky. Some of our colleagues elsewhere ended up sleeping rough and eating cold army rations.

This area was very definitely Inkhatha. As we come under the railway bridge into Sundumbili I noticed the word *Shenge* painted large on each side. That was a praise name for Chief Buthelezi. I told the men to make no jokes about him. Later while touring the district I noticed a hillside that had recently had a couple of dozen houses on it, but they had been burned down. It had been lived in by ANC activists who had been a bit too active and irritated their neighbours.

Breakfast at their canteen was huge. Few of us ever managed to finish a whole meal as offered. We had to contend with half chickens, big steaks, piles of putu and vegetables plus puddings; and if we were around between meals they would anxiously bring us plates of sandwiches. Compared with SAP rations which were army dog packs, this was luxury.

The KZP station commander, Major Zuma, arrived. He asked, after checking who and how many we were, if we needed anything. He was rather cheered when I asked for shotguns and forty rounds each for half my people, so that all nine had either a rifle or shotgun in addition to a sidearm and gas. There had been problems at three of the ten voting sites in that district on the first day, so three of my members went to each to stiffen the police presence which was rather thin, say two or three men armed only with R3 rifles but no gas or sidearms or batons to control several hundred if not thousands of locals.

I went off in a VW Golf with a local KZP W/O and our computer boffin to tour all the polling stations in the magisterial district, which was about 35km square of largely steep hill country with a few dirt roads – well, dirt unless bedrock. A couple of times our driver stopped to work out how to get down or across the road. The polling stations were nearly all schools, small primary schools with minimal if any equipment or furniture, no running water, the grounds a sloping hillside grazed by the local goats, the office two drawers in the headmaster's desk which itself was in the corner of a classroom, and often little plaques over classroom doors naming donors from America or Europe.

There were observers from all over: the UN, the Electoral Commission, the Pennsylvanian Baptist Church, the BBC, etc.

etc. We strolled about, talked to the electoral officers (generally the headmasters), checking they had enough voting papers and no crowd or other problems.

I also chatted to various observers. An Irish author hired by the UN (not for the first time, as it was his winter job), reckoned the UN was an organisational shambles. I showed him broadly how stick fighting worked using some left at the entrance. Two sticks, one the lighter parrying stick, the other the heavy hitting knobkierie, were treated as dangerous weapons. A teacher politely told me that the light stick I had picked up was an old lady's stick. The female UN type saw my demonstration and fled back indoors. When I later asked her what statistics she was noting, she clutched her clipboard fiercely to her chest, glared at me (clearly viewing me as a horned devil or brutal agent of the repressive regime), and scuttled off, which vastly amused her colleague.

One black US Baptist reduced my black colleagues to giggles: they thought him a complete idiot. All he lacked was a cap with a propeller on it.

The BBC news producer, there with a camera crew, was very surprised to find that most locals knew more about English first division soccer than he did. He then asked which team I supported. When I replied Wimbledon, then in their improbable prime, as they played like a bunch of eager six year olds, it turned out he lived there but had never watched them.

My troops were seriously thirsty at their posts: no safe water, no food, a hot Zululand day with a berg wind and sand storms. I dropped off two-litre bottles of cool drinks and took orders for drinks. We managed to find an open bottle store in Mandini and loaded up. That evening all fifteen of us had a serious party. One of my youngsters, who rejoiced in the name of Van Buren Scheele, tried against all advice to keep up with me on the whisky. He spent most of the next day face down on a slab of concrete. I remember toddling very gently through to the dormitory at 6 am and asking if anyone had any tea. Don Vermoter, a battle-hardened veteran sergeant, just replied, "Go back to sleep sir". So I did, sitting upright.

Fortunately we were held in reserve at the station on day three, so we drank tea, nibbled the sandwiches brought every hour, and watched the cow donated for the next station braai grazing in the backyard. That morning I was talking to the major when he said, "I hear you're an attorney?"

"Yes."

"Oh I may need one soon."

"Why? Are you in the shit?"

There was a profound silence while the local lieutenant of detectives wished he could vanish. Later I heard a rumour that the major had fourteen murder charges being investigated against him. I subsequently met him after he had been transferred to Area HQ, and he was full of the joys of life.

Mind you, they had a pretty brisk way of dealing with problems. For no obvious reason one of my constables managed to gas the only prisoner in the cells, something totally stupid, unnecessary and against every conceivable regulation. One of the locals stopped any complaint. I gather he walked into the cell, stuck the muzzle of his G3 into the prisoner's mouth, and asked if he wished to make a complaint. It is then very difficult to do anything but shake your head – very carefully.

Day three of the election was calm and we all went home.

Appendix

NOTES ON PRONOUNCIATION AND LANGUAGE

The English spoken in Durban in the period of the 1980s and 1990s had a character somewhat different from that spoken elsewhere in South Africa. Broadly it was more guttural than the versions used in the Cape or Johannesburg. The original settlers from Britain arrived with a variety of local accents. Those in the Eastern Cape who came in 1820 seem to have had an accent not dissimilar to what we today would reckon an Australian one, and this could still be heard in the country districts around Grahamstown or Bathurst until say the 1970s. In Natal the Byrne settlers of 1849 were largely from Scotland and Yorkshire, like my great-grandmother who arrived from Glasgow in the 1850s and kept her Scots till she died at the age of 92. The South African English accent seems to have evolved towards the end of the nineteenth century, and was based on the English spoken in the Home Counties, which was what the official or educated classes spoke; when the Lithuanians took it up the die was cast.

Among the Dutch-speaking population the reverse happened. What they actually spoke was Plattdeutsch, the old common tongue of the area now covered by the Flemish part of Belgium, the Netherlands and the northern half of Germany. Dutch or, as it was commonly known, High Dutch or Hoog Hollands was the language of the pulpit and the officials. After the second English takeover in 1806 this slowly atrophied, and under the impact of the Afrikaans language movement from the 1870s this process accelerated until Afrikaans as a new and distinct language replaced Dutch as an official language in 1925, which was a nuisance for my mother who had to change to it for her last year at school. The earliest written versions were a humorous column in an Eastern Cape newspaper about a certain Kaaitje Kekkelbek and a translation of the Koran written in Arabic script, both dating from the mid-nineteenth century. It had absorbed a lot of Malay, Khoi and Black words, and developed a rhythm quite unlike its European parent as it tended to end off sentences on a rising inflection. It became the home tongue of the Coloureds and the lingua franca for most of the rural areas outside the coastal and midlands areas of Natal and parts of the Eastern Cape. (A similar but more marked process has in passing led in the Dutch Antilles to the language called Papiermenten which has taken up a lot of Spanish.) Of course it absorbed a lot of English words too, such as *orraait* and *horrog*. The latter baffled me when my roomie at Stellenbosch asked me if he could fetch me one. He then described a hot dog.

The English speakers of Durban cheerfully borrowed words from all and sundry, but mostly Afrikaans and Zulu, simply because we all spoke two or three languages. My farming cousins were generally expert Zulu speakers, while city folk were more likely to be able to talk Afrikaans, if not quite chat or understand the jokes. The first thing to note is that we pronounced the guttural "g" rather like a Scot saying the "ch" in *loch*. Though this did not directly affect English words there was a tinge of it. The "i" sound in say *try* or *nice* would be dragged out so that *nice try* could tend towards *naas traai*. Next was the tendency to make the "ch" sound shorter and more explosive as in *tjeers* for *cheers*. Then the sound of a double vowel in borrowed or Afrikanerised words tended to be sounded with a rising then falling inflection, something again cribbed from Afrikaans. *Tjeers* would therefore be *tje-ers*. But then the "r" would be rolled making it *tje-errs*. We seldom said *yes* or *oh*: it was *ja* or *ja-a* or *ja-a?*, and *ag* which gives a trruly disgusted sound. Another sound similarly borrowed was the pronunciation of "v" as "f". A Volkswagen was called a *Volksie*, said *faulksie* not, as the English say it, *vowkswagon*. Many of the words were borrowed simply because they sounded *lekker*. However to go too far in this direction save for comic effect made you sound pretty low class, a bit of a *tang*. This was pioneered in the early 1960s by a very popular musical revue called *Ag Pleez Daddy*. There was still a snobbish attitude among the Hooray Henry or the older English speakers who liked to consider Afrikaners lower class or poor whites, though this was diminishing as the latter worked their way up the business and social ladders. There was also a more pernicious form of self-delusion that "us chaps were right minded and liberal, not like those ghastly racist Afrikaans people". That was the view of the "swimming pool liberals", who were viewed cynically by the rest of us.

When Zulu words are used there are other problems. First, there are the three clicks. The lightest is the "c" as in the surname *Cele*, which is made by the tip of the tongue just behind the top front teeth. Next is the one made by the tip of the tongue against the roof of the mouth as in *Xhosa* or *Ixopo*, which was said to be the sound of a rock being dropped in a river. The last is made with the side of the tongue and the side of the mouth as in *Nqutu* or the tongue twister surname *Nqonqwane*. There are several variants of these three basic clicks, but do not ask me to dissert. Unlike English you do not pronounce a word or syllable ending with an "e" as one. *Pelele* is thus *pe-le-le*. That means "finished". A "ph", in passing, is an explosive "p".

Just to complicate things of course, the bulk of those in Durban who spoke English as a first language were the Indians, whose accents ranged from international standard academic to the rapid-fire style memorably described by one tourist as sounding just like Peter Sellers. This tended to leave out both articles and personal pronouns and curiously used more Afrikaans words than most Whites would.

I have set out below a list of some of the more obvious Durban usages that were not standard or English-English, both borrowings and local meanings. These were pretty well normal throughout the country but would not necessarily be so well used or understood in say Pretoria or Vryburg. To help with pronunciation among other aspects, I have shown the derivation with an A for Afrikaans, Z for Zulu and I for Indian, which embraces Hindi, Tamil and all others.

Africa used in the phrase "for Africa" – as in "He's got cars for Africa" – meant an awful lot; cf the English "shedloads"

Amandla (Z) power, specifically Black power; often used as a shout during protests

Aryan in Durban this referred to Indians only, as in the Aryan Benevolent Society

Atjar (A fr Malay) pickled vegetables, e.g. limes; used like chutneys as a side dish or sauce

Avo short for avocado pear; in Durban a common garden fruit

Babbelaas (A) to be hung over, as in "He's got a helse babbelaas"

Bad attitude this covered a wide range from surly to argumentative to dumb insolence

Bak (A) a term of approval, also bakgat

Bakkie (A) a pickup or LDV, the universal farmers' vehicle with or without a canopy. There were no vans or transit vans, so nearly all tradesmen used them as did the police, who used ones with steel canopies with mesh sides and a solid steel door at the rear

Ballie (A) as in "an old ballie", referred to an older man at least one generation older than the speaker

Beerhall specifically a hall, generally municipally owned, where juba was sold, only to Blacks: generally large with seating for hundreds. One old one near the beachfront, in my time a panelbeater's, also had six huge fireplaces along each side, each big enough to roast a whole ox. It was used as a temporary mortuary during the 1949 riots

Bell me telephone me, a convergence with the Afrikaans bel my

Berg wind the hot and very dry wind that blows down from the Drakensberg, which tops 3,000m, to the Midlands or the coast. I have known it raise the temperature by 10°C in less than an hour

Beskuit a rusk, commonly eaten with coffee; my favourite types are raisin or buttermilk

Biltong dried meat prepared in stiff sun-dried strips then sliced; most commonly beef but also kudu, springbok and even ostrich; similar to the American jerky. Droewors was a dried sausage that served as a savoury snack with beer or wine

Bioscope an older name for a cinema, then falling out of use; hence bio and café-bio

Blacks this term certainly referred to Black Africans; whether it included Indians or Coloureds was open to debate, largely on political grounds. Self-styled progressives tended to say it did; conservatives – which included many Blacks – tended to disagree. The Afrikaans equivalent, swartes, did not include any non-blacks. This term did not distinguish between the various tribes or between local or foreign. In Durban nearly all of them were Zulu

Blompotte (A) flowerpots; a derisory nickname used by the SAP for the old SA Railways Police constables, as they sat around in the sun on platforms

Blue train methylated spirits, drunk by the truly desperate. It gives a very distinctive and revolting bad breath

the Bluff the name of the long spit that formed the southern shore of Durban bay. Originally used for a whaling station, railway depot and oil storage farm, it attracted – by reputation – a rather rough type of resident. It felt rather remote, like an offshore island

Bobotie (A fr Malay) a form of curried meatloaf, normally with raisins, apple or other fruit and turmeric; very rootsy

Boerewors (A) also boerrie or wors; the definitive SA sausage, it must contain coriander but the rest relies on the maker's taste or lack of it. Generally based on beef or mutton (but not pork), but every butcher has his own recipe. Needs to be quite fatty to feed the coals on a braai

Boff short form of boffin, someone clever; known in Wales as a brainbocs

Bossies to be battle-happy or slightly deranged; cf bosbefok as in "don't mess with those Recces, they're seriously bossies".

Bottle store a shop selling liquor; originally only a licensed hotel could operate one and to be a hotel the premises had to have twelve rooms. Most country hotels relied heavily on their liquor sales as very possibly there was no other outlet within thirty kms

Breker (A) pr brre-e-kerr; a hard man, a tough guy

Braai (A) pr bry; the all-South-African meal: wors and meat cooked over hot coals, the one meal that the men cook; a posh one may use vine stumps, but it can be done, at a pinch, with paper in a bucket. Refers also to the grids or construction, and to the act of grilling.

Bread, a a loaf of bread, as in "getting a bread and a milk"; nearly always white as you can eat that straight without any butter or spreads

Bra fr brother, pr brah, as in "howzit my bra?"

Bredie (A) pr bre-edie; a stew commonly involving mutton and sugar, often cooked at a braai in a three-legged pot, the old kaffirpot, but stirred. One classic is waterblommetjiebredie, made with mutton and a type of water lily found in the Boland.

Breyani (I) a type of curry of spiced rice with meat or occasionally fish. The rice in posh versions may be cooked in three or four colours then placed in the serving dish in shapes, giving an effect like an artistic rainbow cake. This was reckoned the best form of curry

Brinjal an aubergine or eggplant, probably from Anglo-Indian fr Portuguese

Bunnychow (from I) from bahnia chow, businessman's meal; a quarter, half or whole white loaf hollowed out, filled with curry and with the inside of the loaf put back on top: hence beefbunny, veggiebunny, or – direly – a greasebunny

Bush, the the bushveld; an large area in the northwestern Transvaal of dry grassland with thorn trees seldom more than seven metres tall; traditionally good hunting country

Buster a form of line squall that came up Natal coastal waters. The wind can go from a calm to 40 knots or more in seconds, enough to knock down a sailing ship

By quite often used where the usual English preposition would be "to"; as in "Going by pozzie?"

Café often pr kef-fee; this word was applied to virtually any sort of corner shop that sold food or groceries. It might sell takeaway tea but you'd be amazed to find a table and chairs

Cane pr kayne; as in "cane for the pain"; cane spirit or industrial-grade Bacardi

Car guard the guy who stopped your car from being damaged when you parked. More importantly, he would feed your parking meter before the meter maid reached it

Charro (?) an Indian; a neutral term – if you want a fight, try "coolie"

Castle, a the most popular SA lager. Basically all local beers were lagers, barring a couple of stouts and an urbok from Windhoek, and were drunk chilled

China fr china plate, a mate; pr tjina

Chips potato chips or crisps. The French-fry type is often known as slap tjips and all too often lived up to that name

Chorb a pustule generally arising from a blackhead or whitehead; cf the US term "zit"

Chow food or a meal, or to eat, as in "D'you want a chow?"

Clip a slang term for a hundred rand

Coloureds this group included a number of disparate groups, but the basic and largest component came from a Hottentot or Khoisan base with a sizeable admixture of White, Malay, Indian, Bushman or San and Black blood. By default anyone who did not qualify for one of the other three groups had to be Coloured. The Malays and Griquas were perhaps the two biggest distinct communities, kept together by history and religion in certain areas in the Cape, as were the Reheboth Basters up in the old SWA; but racially they tended to shade into the White, Black and Indian groups. Culturally most were part of the Afrikaans community by language, religion and social habits, but were stereotyped as the more spontaneous or feckless part, as opposed to the dour and worthy Calvinist self-image of the Blankes. The Malays were Muslim but the rest were largely Christian. Socially the Coloured guys in the police reserve were closer to the White or Indian members, which was in part because we all spoke English, notwithstanding surnames like Boomgaard or Geschwindt

Come right sort yourself out, as in, "you have a bad attitude, you must make sharp and come right"

Connection someone known, either a friend or patron

Cool drink the general name for any canned or bottled non-alcoholic drinks

Corrugations the name for the ridges running across dirt roads at roughly right angles to the line of the road, caused by the harmonic qualities of the soil or clay making up the road surface. The way to counter their impact, which can throw a vehicle off the road, is either to slow right down or to speed up so that the tyres only hit the tops of the ridges. Occasionally one finds ridges of sand or stones running lengthwise: these are known as corduroy; and are also dangerous especially on curves

Cause crabs to be a bloody nuisance, or to create problems, as in "that skollie is only causing crabs"

Customary marriage also known as tribal rites; a form of marriage open to Blacks. Though the form of the ceremony and the payment of lobola varied from tribe to tribe, broadly it allowed polygamy with no limit in numbers, the return of an infertile wife against a refund of the lobola, or alternatively the supply of a younger sister as a shadow wife. Traditionally if a man died his oldest surviving brother was obliged to marry his widow(s). This was in some ways in conflict with the Christian or civil marriage which was fully recognised by the law, unlike the customary, which in those days was recognised fully only for third party claimants for personal injury in motor collisions

Dagga (Khoisan) cannabis or marijuana, aka Durban poison or zol. Given the chance it can grow to a tree ten metres or more high, but is best treated like a tea bush and kept to, say, two metres and the leaves plucked when just uncurling. Traditionally smoked by old Zulus to ease their rheumatism

Dik thick or dull-witted

Dof soft in the head; as in "he's real dof"

Dom stupid; as in "dom, dik and difficult"

Dompas literally "stupid pass", the name used by everyone for the passbook carried previously by all Black, i.e. African, people. It was the focus for much resentment. In theory they had to carry it at all times but this was in Durban largely unenforceable, even assuming that the police wanted to try. I remember only one operation in about 1983 when a sweep was made of Black servants/staff quarters to find undesirables. The main result was reports to the city council against the owners for substandard and overcrowded premises.

Later they were abolished and replaced with identity books, the same as for everyone else

Donga (A) a washed-out rainwater gully, the result of erosion caused by a lack of ground cover from overgrazing. I have seen examples as deep as six or eight metres. On a large scale the veld is reduced to a moonscape with no topsoil and even thorn trees washed away. Goats are the biggest single cause

Doos literally a box, but really means a bloody fool. In Afrikaans a very rude word, but less so in English

Dop a tot of liquor. The dop system in the winelands meant the workers were paid in part with wine, which led to a lot of drunkenness on Fridays and weekend

Doppie a cartridge case; 9mm doppies made good impromptu earplugs

Durbs pr duhbz; the local slang term for Durban; also sometimes Durbs-by-the-sea

Eina pr ey-NAH; ouch

Ek se pr ek-sey; lit. I say; a self-important personage, roughly the same as the English phrase "the great I am"; as in, "That is one painful ek se"

Europeans this meant white people, plus Japanese who on commercial grounds were given honorary status. The local Chinese were not, and had a little Group Area in Port Elizabeth. Elsewhere they were more or less unofficially part of the Whites, and went to White private schools; though when the student vice-chairman of the UCT Law Society in 1970 was Chinese, the Pig and Whistle pub in Cape Town refused to cater for the joint UCT/Stellenbosch dinner. It was switched to Tollies in Stellenbosch, then owned by Prof Nic Olivier, a prominent verligte Nationalist

Ey hey without an h

Ewe (Z) pr eh-weh; yes. The word for no is Xa

Fanagolo a hybrid language based primarily on Zulu and Xhosa; developed on the mines as a lingua franca for the Black recruits who came from all over Southern Africa. The rough and ready household equivalent was traditionally known as kitchen kaffir

Farm, the term used by Zulus to describe a family's rural home or Kraal as in "Who was last at the farm?" Hence the use of "farm boy" to indicate a rustic

Fighting sticks a traditional Zulu weapon consisting of a light stick as a defence and a knobkierie for attack. The only weapon that could stop a stick fighter was a firearm

Film pr fill-um; again a blurring with Afrikaans; cf flicks pr fleeks

Finish and klaar a tautological phrase meaning something is irreversibly finished

Floppy a terrorist who flops over when shot, as in slotting a floppy: a Rhodesian term

Flymasjini (Z) an aeroplane, mostly used in joke

Foofy slide fr the Afrikaans foefie, a handle or bar or some such on a pulley wheel that rolls or slides down a long wire cable attached to a tree or other high point falling gradually to the ground or another tree, known in England as a zip wire

Fundi (fr Z) fr ifundisi, an expert

Gammadoelas (A) pronounced with a guttural g, the back of beyond, or beyond the black stump

Gat (A) a hole, as in slaggat or pothole; or in slang usage an arsehole. Derived from this were many descriptive terms such as slapgat for lazy, gatslag for a misfortune, windgat for pretentious, ingat for introvert, or vuilgat for someone who tells really dirty stories, which most likely came in from army slang

Gavine (Z) a homebrewed concoction made by Blacks. I have seen it brewing in a 44-gallon drum, grey and slowly bubbling. Traditionally suspected of using dead dogs, battery acid, bicycle tyres and other less savoury items. Occasionally lethal.

Graft work, but seldom if ever used in the sense of corrupt activities; as when I asked a mortuary cop how he liked it there, he replied it was lekker graft.

Grafting working, in a neutral sense: as in "Ey you busy?" "Yes, grafting man grafting."

Graze to eat or the food itself as in: "Let's go by the café and get some graze": cf chow

Gumboot a rubber Wellington boot, associated with the miners' gumboot dances

Gundagunda (Z) fr the sound, a steamroller

Harraharra a mocking laugh useful at political meetings or other lively occasions

Hash fr hashish; a concentrate of dagga that looks a bit like an OXO cube, uncommon, as not made locally, mostly found on foreign ships or yachts

Helse (A) helluva

Houtie or *houtkop (A)* a woodenhead, used mostly of Blacks though not as a general term of abuse, cf the English term woodentop

Houseboy obsolescent word for a Black male house servant. My grandmother had one called John in the 1950s, whose worst job was polishing the verandahs with sticky red polish.

Howsit or hazzit short for how's it going?

Hudeni (Z) lit heathen; this was used of the animist/traditionalist Zulus from the remote rural areas such as Msinga or Tugela Ferry who would turn up in crowds, even in Colenso in the early 1960s, for Christmas shopping, the married women dressed in traditional leather skirts, clay headdresses etc, the unmarried girls in short skirts and little else, decked out with all sorts of decorations, even red plastic fly swatters. The Christian Zulus correctly referred to them as kaffirs

Indians this group consisted of people who had immigrated from India since the 1850s. The bulk came as indentured labourers to labour on sugar cane farms in the Natal coastal strip and were either Hindus, largely from the Bombay side, or Tamils from the Madras or eastern side of India. There were also a number of passenger Indians (so called as they paid their own fares), who were largely business or professional types such as a certain adv Gandhi. As a group they were very ambitious, set up and funded schools all over Natal, spread into market gardening and small retail, such as the vegetable sammies, then bigger businesses of all sorts. Although there were still rag pickers and labourers among them, a large slice of the professional and wealthy side of Durban was Indian. When Harold Macmillan visited in 1960, the local English-speaking establishment borrowed the best car in town from an Indian businessman to take him around, but refused to invite him to the Whites-only dinner. In my time the largest group in the prosecutors' pool at the magistrates' courts became Indian women, while the top neurosurgeon was Indian. One of my fellow cricket umpires by name of Khan reckoned his was the only Pathan family in town, his grandfather having come over to make umbrellas

Induna (Z) a head man over a number of kraals, he was below the chief in rank, but served as his representative. In tribal areas he could assign land for kraals or houses. In towns he was the head of a ward and had considerable influence.

Ja-well-no-fine a useful phrase that means, basically but not definitively, umm

Jissus fr Jesus pr yes-sus also simply yus an exclamation of surprise; as in Oh jissus you gave me a skrik (ie a fright)

Jol (A) a party or to party; hence joller = a party animal

Juba (Z) fr ijuba, beer made from sorghum (previously called kaffir corn); sold in one- or two-litre cartons left with a small opening at the top to allow it to froth out, after which it was drunk. An acquired taste as it tastes like milk of magnesia; but was a very useful vitamin additive for a maize-based diet

Kapie pr k-p, someone from the Cape Province and more particularly the Western Cape; could also be used for a Coloured; cf klong

Kazzie fr cousin; a friend or acquaintance; cf gabba poss A

Khehla (Z) an old man in a respectful sense, pr kethla At Michaelhouse Old Boys' meetings the oldest old boy present is named as the khehla

Klap (A) a blow with the flat of the hand to the face or head; hence a tight klap or a stiff klap. Often strong enough to knock one down. Can also burst an ear drum

Koeksusters (A) a type of sweetmeat made of two plaited squared strips of dough, crisped then soaked in a light syrup. Very more-ish with coffee but definitely a home baker's speciality, as they should be eaten fresh and slightly crisp

Laaitjie (A) pr lie-tee a boy or son; as in "A man must have a laaitjie"

Laatlammetjie (A) pr la-atlammikie; lit a late little lamb; the youngest child in a family, especially one five or ten years younger than the others

Lahnie (I) someone rich, as in "Ey lahnie, see us right with a cane"

Lapa (?Tswana) a place to meet to discuss or socialise. The lapa at Dewetskop grew around a braai in the lee of a couple of buildings with space to sit or mingle and could hold fifty or more

Late a euphemism for dead, but used largely by Blacks or Indians as in "My sister she is late"

Lekker (A) nice or good; also pr luckus

Lobola (Z) the bride price paid under customary law by the bridegroom to the bride's father. This was paid also in civil or Christian marriages. For commoners it was five cattle or the cash equivalent, which for a town-based labourer was six or nine months' wages. A chief or induna might demand forty head but a royal bride could well cost 400 head of cattle.

In a divorce the husband could recover the lobola less one cow for each child born

Long Tom the nickname for the larger so-called quart bottles of beer, as opposed to the standard 340ml bottles; probably derived from the name of a Boer artillery piece used to defend Lydenburg in 1900 which gave its name to the Long Tom Pass

Luck a woman of negotiable virtue; as in "You think I'm a luck?"

Maid In local terms a Black servant, though the Afrikaans equivalent meid referred specifically to a Coloured: a black would be called a (huis) bediende

Make sharp hurry up

Mampoer(A) peach brandy famously made around Rustenburg by a few dozen licensed still owners; and many others

Man referred to either a man or a woman, as in "Ag man don't be like that ey!"

Mampara (?) pr with the accent on the second a; a term of abuse for someone dim and clueless

Mandrax a drug, an upper used commonly in powder form and smoked mixed with dagga in a so-called white pipe: long use gives you a condition similar to miner's phthisis

Mbela (Z) the porridge made from sorghum, dark brown in colour, nutty and sweet in flavour

Mealies the local word for maize or corn on the cob; stampmielies or samp was crushed dry maize commonly boiled as a vegetable, especially by Blacks

Mlungu (Z) pl Abalungu; a white man

Moegoe (A) pr mu-ghu; another bloody fool

Moer (A) pr moor; two uses, the first to hit or beat up as in I'll moer you: the second the equivalent of the "c" word but not used as a description, rather as in the abusive challenge Jou ma se moer, or, Gaan vlieg in jou moer in, often shortened to just Gaan vlieg (literally go fly)

Moerig (A) upset or annoyed

Moffie (A) a homosexual; a Cape term referring to the mincing queen type as a rule

Muggie (A) a small persistent fly that comes in clusters and serves the same annoying role as the Scottish midge or the Arctic mosquito

Muti (Z) medicine as used by herbalists or witch doctors: ranges from herbal remedies to human body parts used to give strength, etc

Naartjie (A) a citrus fruit with a very loose skin traditionally eaten by spectators at rugby matches, sometimes after they were injected with brandy. The peel or perhaps the whole fruit was occasionally thrown at the referee

Nkosi (Z) a chief or lord, used also in Christian language for the Lord, as in the national anthem, which was written in the nineteenth century as a hymn

Non-Europeans meant anyone other than Whites. Foreigners such as Filipino seamen in Durban tended to go to certain specific nightclubs and bars which everyone including the police recognised as de facto mixed, wherever they happened to be. Rich foreigners went to the Royal Hotel or the Edward. In Durban the strict barriers eroded steadily over time in advance of the abolition of the statutes such as the Group Areas Act.

Now the great SA mystery word, it means soonish, but must be distinguished from just now which is not so quick, and now-now which means just now in the English sense but not right now. This is the result of a blurring with the Afrikaans words nou and nou-nou

Numzaan (Z) strictly speaking the head of a kraal, roughly equivalent to the Roman paterfamilias, but used colloquially to mean sir. I would commonly be addressed with this when greeted in Zulu

Nunu (Z) literally a small insect or songololo; but used figuratively for the penis of a small boy

APPENDIX

Okapi a clasp knife with a blade about 15cm long, being the name of a very common cheap make

Oke (A) fr outjie, roughly the equivalent of a bloke, but does not suggest anyone unduly dignified

Oom (A) an uncle, but used by Afrikaners to address an older man as a sign of respect. I was first addressed as oom when I was fourteen which made me feel instantly aged. The female equivalent was tannie. To talk of the oomies at the bowling club would be mostly friendly but possibly with a tinge of disdain. A soustannie (literally a "sauce aunt"), was a gossipy old lady

Only used instead of very or extremely, as in "That was only gross"

Out, an a vagrant or person of no fixed abode, but almost certainly ragged and dirty and probably with drink or mental problems

Pain when used as a verb was a Charro usage, as in "I am paining paining"

Pal often pr pel or pellie

Panga (Z) a cane knife with a heavy metal blade normally about 90cm long and 7/8 cms wide with a hooked tip. It makes a vicious weapon in a fight. Basically the same as a machete

Passion gap this was formed by pulling the four front teeth in the upper jaw presumably to make a French kiss into something more absorbing; among other things. Largely confined to Coloured working-class people, and probably declining as a habit. Makes for a memorable smile

Peppercorn hair this was the distribution of hair on the head in little spots, themselves often in groups of say half a dozen each, separated by bare skin. The hairs are very crinkly and tend to break off short. This is a sure sign of Bushman blood and is commonest among Griquas and Hlubis in the Eastern Cape

Petrol jockey the person at a garage who filled your tank, pumped your tyres, cleaned your windscreen, etc. I never had to put in petrol in years

Pie pr paai, but still a pie

Piccanin (Z) a small Black boy. A girl was an intombezaan

Piccanin kia (Z) lit the small house; an outside toilet or longdrop; often simply PK

Pick 'n Pray the local name for a large evangelical church in Durban North next to the Pick 'n Pay hypermarket

Plan, make a plan cf A " 'n boer maak n plan": what it says, but with elements of self-reliance and resourcefulness, or when used as an exhortation implies get on with it

Poking stabbing, as in "He was poking me with his Okapi"

Pomp (A) literally a pump but in reality definitely not. The ability to tell a pomp from a pump was one essential skill for a plumber. Generally what was done to a punda

Pondok (Z) a shack built of anything available eg large crates, plastic sheeting, corrugated iron, or juba cartons filled with earth and mounted on a frame of say reinforcing rods. One could be thrown up overnight. Also called an mjondolo. A traditional beehive hut was made of a framework of saplings making a hemisphere with grass mats over it, and was portable

Porro, alt Porra a Portuguese; neutral, but depended how you said it. There were said to be more Madeirans in SA than in Madeira

Potjie (A) pr poy-key; a dish cooked slowly and unstirred in an iron three-legged pot over coals at a braai. The trick is to layer the pot to prevent burning. One classic recipe is fatty mutton and pumpkin in alternating layers with a bit of cinnamon

Pozzie (?) a house or home

Pro Nutro a form of breakfast cereal developed in the 1960s as a source of vitamins and proteins to combat Kwashiorkor, a vitamin-deficiency condition that gave Black children ginger-coloured hair among other problems. Later it was the nickname for the Pro Patria medal given to troops who had been on active service in the border war for 90 days

Punda (?) a vagina or more generally sex, as in the okes are going out looking for punda. By an unhappy chance the point next the harbour at Willemstad in Curacoa with all the government offices has this name

Put foot to accelerate fast, of a vehicle

Putting pleasure by the body one way to describe sex, usually used by Indians

Putu (Z) maizemeal porridge commonly made dry and eaten with gravy or tomato and onion sauce especially at braais where it is virtually obligatory. Everybody eats it. Also called stywe pap, ie stiff porridge

Recce a member of the Reconnaissance Battalion, a special forces unit that specialised in long-range penetration behind enemy lines in Angola and even, by report, Tanzania, to gather intelligence or observe artillery strikes. They had a base on the Bluff.

Retread either a vehicle tyre revulcanised, but often illegally and thus very dangerous; or of a person of similar qualities; not a word of praise

Robots traffic lights; sometimes pr row-bows

Rock spider a derogatory Natal term for a Vaalie, often simply a "rock": very much not the English usage. "Can you speak rock?" "Speaking in code" also referred to Afrikaans.

Rods trousers; underpants were called underrods

Rof (A) rough; sometimes a deliberate mispronounciation for comic effect; as in "We're rof and we're tof, and we come from the Bloff"

Rondavel (A) a circular hut originally with walls of wattle and daub with a thatched roof; hence a square hut is a square-davel

Rubbish, a someone of no value or values; cf A vullis (pr phyllis) as in "Those rubbishes next door"

S and T Snot and Tears, fr A snot en trane; a description of emotional movies; cf weepies

Sarnie a sandwich

Sambals (I) side dishes served with curry; eg chopped tomato, onion, and peppers, or grated coconut.

Sammy (I) a hawker. The Indian market gardeners used to sell their produce door to door, initially (pre-war) from a couple of baskets slung from a carrying pole, but later from bakkies

Sangoma (Z) a herbalist/witchdoctor; can be male or female and in traditional society fills the roles of doctor, psychiatrist, clairvoyant and social worker. Their muti can fix your love life and your sporting prowess, and prevent parking tickets. Most Black-run premier league soccer teams reportedly had one on retainer

Sardine Run an annual event when huge shoals of sardines came up the coast from the Cape, hunted all the way by sharks, dolphins and other predators. The shoals would beach themselves at random points along the coast, where people could rush into the surf to catch them with anything available. Oddly, when sold commercially they were called, in English, pilchards

Schlenter a good sounding Yiddish word for a swindle

Schlep another good Yiddish word, this for a hassle

Shad a coastal fish up to two kg, very good eating, often caught just outside the surf line with three to four metre rods casting from the beach

Shame pr shaayme as in "ag shame ey!"; the standard response to babies, roughly the equivalent of "oh cute" or "isn't she sweet"; alternatively an expression of sympathy; cf the English idiom "bless"

Sharp often used to mean good or well; as in "Howsit my bra?" "No, sharp-sharp"

Shebeen an Irish term used specifically for Black drinking venues in the townships, often illegal and normally informal

Shottie a shotgun

Sjambok (A fr Malay) a heavy whip traditionally cut square from rhino hide, about a metre long and about three cm across at the handle tapering to the tip, nowadays made of plastic and sold by vendors on the beachfront.

Skate low class or scummy; as in "That chick is truly skate"

Skollie a crook or gangster, used particularly of Coloureds

Skop, skiet en donder (A) literally "kick, shoot and beat up"; the generic name for action movies, comics etc, originally applied to cowboy films

Skoten (Z) a bad man, used of Zulu crooks

Skyf (A) a cigarette: fr the word for slice

Slap (A) pr slup; limp or soggy as in tjips; of a person limp or idle as in slapgat

Smous (A) a hawker, particularly in the Cape where vis smouse used to sell fish, using a length of dried kelp as a form of trumpet to announce their arrival

Songololo (Z) a millipede, which in Durban could be 15cms long.

Soutie (A) a nickname for English-speaking South Africans, short for soutpiel which means that you have one foot in SA and the other in the UK with the result that the bit in the middle hangs in the sea and gets salted. I first encountered it as the name for the chaplain at Michaelhouse in 1961 when I thought it Zulu and spelled it soti. In the next generation it referred also to those Afrikaners living in Wimbledon and other parts of the UK

Spaanspek (A) a melon similar to a cantaloupe

Spaza an informal shop in a township generally selling basic food and necessities

Spook n Diesel rum and coke; fr A spook a ghost; good for cold weather, as is katembas, a 50/50 mix of coke and rough red wine

Stutut (Z) fr the sound; a scooter or moped

Swartou (A) a Black neutral term: to cause real offence use coon or kaffir: nigger or negro was never used locally, those were very much American terms

Tackies also tekkies; a gym shoe, or in old terms a plimsoll; hence fat tackies were the monster tyres put on a bakkie for stunt driving

Tang (A) literally a pair of pliers; used to denote a rreally basic oke with no claas

Tickey a threepenny piece, which was no longer minted after decimalisation, so obsolescent, save for a long tickey which was a tickey or later a five-cent piece with a length of wire or thread attached used to make cheap phone calls from the old boxes

Through this had an additional use, as in "he hit him through his face", which indicated a very hard blow

Tjap (A) fr the English "chop" which we borrowed from the Chinese; a rubber stamp, the prized possession of the very minor bureaucrat

Tjeers fr cheerio, a friendly goodbye

Tjor (A) an old car; cf clunker; similarly skedonk (A)

Tog pr with a guttural g, like tochh; tog labourers were casual workers taken on by the day usually for simple manual labour

Tokkolok (A) a divinity student or Dutch Reformed minister, fr their way of walking like a beetle, tik-tok-tokkolok. To help matters those students at Stellenbosch in the 1960s used to wear beetle-crusher shoes

Tokolosh (Z) an evil spirit, normally thought of as a short man of say a metre tall with a penis of about the same size. A good way of repelling them when you sleep is to raise your bed on bricks. People are sometimes murdered if thought to be a tokolosh

Tom cash or money, as in "I must get some tom for a chow"

Tonfa (?) a long baton with side piece, used by police primarily for crowd or individual control

Toppie as in "your old toppie", referred to your father

Toughies an abbreviation of tough luck; as is hardies. It does not show any real sympathy; cf tough titty

Township though technically a deeds registry term for any urban development of erven as in Waterkloof Extension 237 District Witbank; generally used to refer to Black townships such as KwaMashu, named after a sugar farmer called Marshall Campbell

Toyi-toyi a form of dance used during street demonstrations consisting of two hops on the left foot with the right knee raised at right angles, then two hops on the right foot with the left knee raised, continued indefinitely. Common chants during this were "Viva ... viva." "Away ... awaaaay."

Vaalie someone unfortunate enough to come from the Transvaal

Varsity the SA contraction of university

Vat hom fluffy (A) "grab him fluffy": a phrase used both to encourage rugby players to tackle or dogs to attack

Verligte (A) literally someone who is enlightened, as opposed to verkrampte which was a limited or narrow minded type. These terms were coined in the 1960s to distinguish left- and right wing White Nationalists. The verligtes realised that Verwoerdian apartheid could not work and tried to create a more realistic policy, but the verkramptes thought it could if carried out properly. A crystallising issue was the proposed creation of a Coloured homeland, which made no sense historically or economically, unless it included Cape Town. District Six was the rock that sank apartheid

Vetkoek (A) a type of deepfried batter cake about the size of your hand, generally filled with jam or mince. The mince ones were popular at rugby matches

Voet in die hoek (A) to accelerate fast; cf "pedal oppie metal"

Voetsak (A) go away, or something like that. Reputedly the one word all SA dogs understand

Waai (A) to go; pr vie; as in the local Indian slang: "Where waai-ing?" "Ey by pozzie."

Whites This group was conceived of as being people of European descent, and this was pretty well true of the British component and other recent immigrants such as Italians, Germans or Portuguese. The Afrikaans bloodlines were not so clear. Basically they were about one-third Dutch, and one-third German, with the balance being one part French Huguenot, one part British, and the third part a mixture of Malay, Angolan, Madagascan and local Black Hottentot or Bushman; initially due to intermarriage in the seventeenth century when one of the best governors, Simon van der Stel, was half Dutch and half Indian, and a certain Maria van de Kaap, a Hottentot woman, married twice to Dutch settlers. Later in the eighteenth and early nineteenth centuries, in the days of slavery, there was a certain amount of sexual activity by the masters, though not – they hoped – by the mistresses. There was a lot of intermarriage after that, with one's racial category being for some as much a matter of social class as of strict blood lines. Before the 1940s, quite a few White-looking Coloureds moved from the Cape to the Transvaal and became accepted as Whites, the so-called try-for-Whites. Many families straddled the racial divide. In the 1970s two high-profile cases were the leader of the Konservatiewe Party (Conservative Party, a very right-wing White political party), Dr Andries Treurnicht, whose first cousin, also a Treurnicht, was a Coloured representative in parliament; and the widow of Dr Hendrik Verwoerd, who was one of the blas [literally, sallow/tanned] or mixed Schoombies from the Karoo, and who in her old age became more and more visibly Coloured or Griqua in appearance while living in the Whites-only enclave of Orania

Witblits (A) literally white flash, some form of spirits, probably raw, possibly home brewed

APPENDIX

With (from A?) often used without any connected word, as in "Are you coming with?" or "Bring your friend with." Possibly an idiom from A: kom saam.

Zol (?) a twist of dagga wrapped in brown paper about the size of a pencil but a bit shorter, enough for a single smoke; generally sold in bundles of twenty: also loosely used for dagga itself

Zulu warrior a drinking song that starts "Hold him down you Zulu warrior, Hold him down you Zulu chief, chief, chief…" The star would do a down-down drink of beer during the chanting of "chief, chief…", and then stamp, raising his foot to head-height and slamming it full force into the ground. A good stamp should shake the ground, and split the drinker's head.

www.ingramcontent.com/pod-product-compliance
Lightning Source LLC
Chambersburg PA
CBHW062137160426
43191CB00014B/2307